ACPL ITEM
3 1833 03342 3481
DISCARDED

332.024 C66w
Cohen, Li
Wealth bu

S0-BXC-739

Wealth Building

A CONSUMER'S GUIDE TO MAKING PROFITABLE –AND COMFORTABLE– INVESTMENT DECISIONS

Lisa A. Cohen
Beverly D. Flaxington

Dearborn
Financial Publishing, Inc.®

Allen County Public Library
900 Webster Street
PO Box 2270
Fort Wayne, IN 46801-2270

This publication is designed to provide accurate and authoritative information in regard to the subject matter covered. It is sold with the understanding that the publisher is not engaged in rendering legal, accounting, or other professional service. If legal advice or other expert assistance is required, the services of a competent professional person should be sought.

Editorial Director: Cynthia A. Zigmund
Managing Editor: Jack Kiburz
Interior Design: Lucy Jenkins
Cover Design: S. Laird Jenkins Corporation
Typesetting: the dotted i

© 1998 by Dearborn Financial Publishing, Inc.®

Published by Dearborn Financial Publishing, Inc.®

All rights reserved. The text of this publication, or any part thereof, may not be reproduced in any manner whatsoever without written permission from the publisher.

Printed in the United States of America

98 99 00 10 9 8 7 6 5 4 3 2 1

Library of Congress Cataloging-in-Publication Data

Cohen, Lisa A.
    Wealthbuilding : a consumer's guide to making profitable — and
comfortable — investment decisions / by Lisa A. Cohen and Beverly D. Flaxington.
      p.   cm.
    Includes index.
    ISBN 0-7931-2837-4 (pbk.)
    1. Finance, Personal. 2. Investments. 3. Retirement income.
I. Flaxington, Beverly D. II. Title.
HG179.C665   1998
332.024'01—dc21   98-13581
                                             CIP

Dearborn books are available at special quantity discounts to use as premiums and sales promotions, or for use in corporate training programs. For more information, please call the Special Sales Manager at 800-621-9621, ext. 4384, or write to Dearborn Financial Publishing, Inc., 155 North Wacker Drive, Chicago, IL 60606-1719.

Contents

Preface

Have you ever made a list of things that you'd like to learn about and become more comfortable with? Perhaps some of the items on the list are just for fun. Others may be important to your overall well-being. Handling your financial life well and making good investment choices is essential to your financial comfort. Knowing how to make sound, profitable, and comfortable investment and financial decisions is your logical first step.

This issue impacts every one of us, regardless of the size of our pocketbooks. Increasingly, the responsibility for managing money to meet personal goals is falling into our own hands. We're bombarded with messages about the rising costs of education, retirement, and health care. At the same time, traditional cushions like Social Security and company retirement plans are slowly but surely being pulled out from under us. Against this backdrop, more investment information and news are available—Web sites, books, newsletters, magazines, TV shows, and the like—than ever before. The result is what we affectionately call "analysis paralysis." Many people simply stop seeking the information they need to make educated decisions because they become overwhelmed by options and advice. Adding to the problem, the investment industry is steeped in jargon and buzzwords. For most of us, that only increases our level of anxiety about the topic of investing. Not only, we think to ourselves, is the information new, but we also practically have to learn a new language to understand anything the professionals are saying.

Another aggravating factor for a lot of people is "math phobia." The investment business, of course, is about numbers and calculations. Many of us (the authors included) stayed as far away from math classes as we possibly could. But in order to invest wisely, you must understand how to calculate rates of return and figure out what the net costs and benefits of a particular investment will be.

So, if you now realize that knowledge about investing wisely is not going to magically leap into your head, you probably also realize that reading everything available on the topic of investing is as impractical as is ignoring it altogether. We often hear people complain, not about the lack of information available, but about information overload. People ask, "How do I distinguish the useful information from everything that's out there?" The answer, and the reason we have written this book, is to create a framework for making sound, comfortable decisions. Once the groundwork has been laid, you'll be able to distinguish the useful information from the other stuff and know what questions you'd really like answered.

We take the topic of investing for your goals very seriously, and we believe that only by helping you to understand what you're doing—and why you're doing it—will you be able to make profitable, and comfortable, investment decisions. How? In this book we tell you what you really need to know to make sound choices, and guide you through working with the new information so you are comfortable applying it to your own investing decisions. This information is included precisely because it is necessary to the decision-making process; information you really need to make the best investment choices. Rather than overwhelming you with everything you could ever know about investing, this book includes only the information that is necessary for you to have in hand to make better investment decisions.

As you work with this book, we urge you to take a relaxed attitude. We think the investment business can be both informative and fun, and we hope you find as you read and explore with us that it is the same for you. You'll get a chance to revisit and learn from what you've done—even mistakes—and be thoughtful about what you'll do next.

Before you start reading, get prepared with a pad of paper, a pen, and any investing materials you have accumulated to date, such as account statements, prospectuses, and the like. You'll need these things to complete some of the exercises in the book—each of which is structured to help you practice making investing and personal financial decisions for yourself.

Remember the chemistry lab in high school? You weren't allowed to work with the combustible materials unless you had a carefully controlled environment, with safety goggles, test tubes, and supervision. And you always had to practice, and practice, and practice again, before you took on anything too dangerous. That type of learning makes very good sense, to practice until you become comfortable. Think of this book as your own personal financial chemistry lab. After you practice what you've learned, you'll feel comfortable making the investing decisions life calls for (and you won't have to worry about accidentally blowing anything up!).

We wish you good luck, good decisions, the time you need to make comfortable choices, and lots and lots of good fortune!

Acknowledgments

While many people made important suggestions to us in the course of developing this book, we would like to thank several people in particular for their more in-depth contributions:

- Albert W. Amandolare, ChFC, CLU
- Roland (Rob) Gray III, Deutch Williams
- Douglas E. Hart, Penobscot Investment Management Co., Inc.
- Frederick W. Schultz III, Beacon Fiduciary Advisors

Special thanks to our friend and supporter Michael C. Slemmer, CFA.

Most importantly, we would like to thank all of the individuals who have asked excellent, insightful, and pointed questions about the process of making investment decisions. We have written this book for you.

PART 1

Achieving Your Financial Goals

It's a funny thing. As children, we are taught to do new things: how to ride a bike, write our letters, say please and thank you. As teenagers, many of us learn to drive a car, establish a savings account, hold a first job. As adults we receive specialized training to do our jobs and to use emerging technologies. Curiously though, navigating a system as complex as our financial and economic world does not traditionally warrant training and education for the people actually using it! We are simply expected, without benefit of any training or experience to guide us, to manage our finances effectively, select the best products for our situations from an array of thousands, and to comfortably explore the often choppy waters of changing financial markets. The emotional elements of financial decision making—how we feel about our choices and goals—is traditionally not part of the process at all. Actually, it's a wonder any of us get where we're going, financially speaking!

It is important to begin the process of financial planning and investment decision making at the beginning, to learn the information you need to know, to practice with the new information, to evaluate the decisions you've already made, and to make the changes that will help you to achieve your goals. Following the natural process of financial decision making—goal setting, followed by information gathering, followed by decision making—we will help you to evaluate your financial approach, and to make the choices and changes you determine are in order. It's your money; you should make the decisions. Together we'll give you the tools to feel good about making your own investing decisions. So let's begin at the beginning, with your financial goals.

Goal Setting

Goals, financial and otherwise, have one thing in common. They simply don't stand a chance of being accomplished unless you take the time to articulate them and plan a strategy for achieving them. People who plan their financial futures accomplish their goals more often than people who simply hope for the best.

Intuitively, you know that people almost never accomplish things of importance completely by chance. Either you pursue clearly defined goals, and know how well you have performed by whether or not you reach those goals, or you don't plan, allow yourself to be buffeted by the vagaries of the financial world, and never know how well you're doing because you have no goal to measure against.

Buy-in is important too; commitment to the goals must be shared by everyone involved. If that's not the case, the support you need when your goals are challenged (and all goals face challenges), simply won't be there. For that reason, try to complete the exercises in this book with the person or people who will be affected by your hopes, goals, and dreams, and include their goals in your thinking, too.

Financial goals are a double-edged sword for many people. On the one hand, they are easy to deal with because they are measurable. I want to save $2,000 by next January for a vacation someplace warm, for example. At the same time, financial goals are terribly emotional things; we can have very strong feelings about our ability or inability to meet our goals. The emotional piece of the financial goal-setting process is often overlooked; this book will help you to think about that aspect of the financial planning process.

The great news is that the process of accomplishing financial goals can be clearly defined and shared with you, our reader. Once you see how simple the process is, and how much it helps you achieve, you'll feel confident doing it for yourself. The process follows these four steps, each of which we'll talk about and work with in detail:

1. Identify your financial goals.
2. Establish specific dollar amounts for goals.
3. Set time frames for achieving your goals.
4. Evaluate and confirm financial priorities.

For most of us, financial goals are simple. They involve reducing debt, moving to a bigger house, starting a business, or paying for our kids' educations. Some of us have grander schemes. Whatever your goal, simple or wildly extravagant, planning will make the difference between just having a dream of going to graduate school or the reality of inviting the family over for a graduation party.

Identify Your Personal Financial Goals

Naturally, the first step in setting and achieving your goals is to state them clearly. Financial goals can be broken into several broad categories: education, housing, travel and entertainment, general lifestyle (i.e., everything from new cars or landscaping to owning your own business or even being independently wealthy), and, of course, the biggest financial goal for most of us, retirement. You may want to organize your goals this way. You also may have financial goals that don't fit into one of these categories—that's fine, too.

- Education
- Housing
- Travel and entertainment
- Lifestyle
- Wealthbuilding
- Retirement
- Other things that are important to you!

Goals and Values

Financial goals are intimately linked to values, to what we believe to be important and worthwhile. Because we tend to focus our energies on the goals

5

we value most, we also tend to accomplish them. What does this mean to you? If you are working toward financial goals that are *not* linked to your values, it is less likely that you will reach them. At the same time, if your financial goals are a part of who you are, of what you value most, you will most likely prioritize and achieve them. Later in this chapter we'll focus on setting practical goals and prioritizing them, keeping in mind your values.

Although you may question the point of this part of the process, this really is the first step in establishing an investment strategy for yourself. Once you have set goals and established time frames for reaching them, developing an investment approach that will support the process is the logical next step. We'll talk in detail about how all this fits together later in the book.

Another critical piece to the goal-setting process is envisioning what your life will be like when you have reached your goal. See yourself at your child's college graduation, or enjoying a comfortable retirement, or taking that trip

News Note

New York Times August 2, 1997
Excerpted from a story by Dirk Johnson

Few people at Chicago Children's Memorial Hospital knew her name. She was simply "The Teddy Bear Lady," the sweet old woman who brought stuffed animals to sick children and vowed to leave a "special gift" to the hospital someday. The woman was a retired secretary who never earned more than $15,000 a year, never married, and lived alone in a tiny apartment in suburban Evanston. But she was more than just sweet. In her will, she left $18 million to Children's Memorial Hospital, the largest single donation in the institution's 115-year history. Miss Holm had been buying stocks for a long, long time. (Copyright © 1997 by the New York Times Co. Reprinted by Permission.)

Financial Goal-Setting Exercise

To kick off the financial goal setting process, brainstorm a list of the things that are important to you financially, that you want to achieve and accomplish. You may see that some of your goals overlap, or need to happen at the same time. If that's the case for you, don't worry. We'll talk later about prioritizing goals and give you some tools to help resolve that issue. For now, just get all of the goals down on a piece of paper. Be sure to list only the goals that really mean something to you.

Step One: Brainstorm your personal list of financial goals.

- Take a minute to think about your financial goals and objectives.
- Write down your goals, include those that are already in process as well as those that are still outstanding and that will probably require some planning to achieve. Number them (not in terms of priority) and leave space under each one to fill in later. Be very specific about the goal. As an example, instead of writing "new car," write "pay full price for a brand new Cutlass Supreme."
- Focus your list to no more than five or six key goals.

Step Two: List why each goal is important to you.

- Next to the goal, write a quick summary of why the goal is important to you and what it means to you. What benefit does the accomplishment of this goal offer you? Again, be specific; the "why" for the Cutlass could be that your current car has more than 100,000 miles on it and buying the new Cutlass will offer you the benefit of driving a larger, safer car and having few, if any, repair bills. Be sure you can clearly describe why this specific goal will benefit you. If it is difficult to describe why this specific goal is important, you may want to reconsider it.

(continued)

- Now envision yourself achieving the goal. Because we all have our own way of using our senses to imagine things, this part of the exercise requires that you first put your pen or pencil down and close your eyes. Can you "see" yourself driving the Cutlass? Can you hear the engine purring gently as you cruise down the highway? Use any senses that come easily to you to imagine yourself *after* you have achieved the goal. What do you look like? What do you feel like? What do others say to you? How is your life different and/or better now that you have reached this goal?

- After you've taken two to three minutes to close your eyes and imagine the goal in whatever way you can, open your eyes and write down some of your thoughts. What specific things did you think about when you were doing this piece of the exercise? If you prefer, take this time to draw a picture of the goal and of the impact accomplishing the goal will have on you. You also may want to cut out a picture of your goal from a magazine or book, or take a photograph of the object or "scene" you want to achieve. Being able to visualize the goal is an important step in being able to reach it.

Step Three: Prioritize your goal list.

Now that you've taken the time to imagine each goal and to write down some key thoughts associated with it, you should be able to easily prioritize those goals. Which ones offer the greatest benefits and will give you the best feelings about accomplishing them? Renumber your original list according to priority. Keep this list. When you complete the Achieving Financial Goals Worksheet in Chapter 2, you'll need this information.

It is very important that you share the results of this exercise with anyone else who is affected by the goals and/or the process of saving to achieve them. This exercise will help you identify your values and set your priorities, individually and with others. If your goals affect a person, or people, other than yourself take some time to come up with a mutual statement of benefits for each goal.

• • • • •

around the world. Often people who don't reach their goals, financial and personal, have not been able to clearly "see" their lives post-goal-accomplishment. You must take time to see, feel, and hear yourself in the future enjoying the benefits of reaching your important goal.

A Personal Story

We recently met a young woman named Sherrie Dobbins who wanted to leave her corporate job as a financial analyst with a large firm and become an independent, small-business owner. As part of her planning process, Sherrie wrote a paragraph about why this goal was important to her and what her life would be like once she achieved the goal. She set time frames and dollar amounts associated with this goal. Sherrie could explain to anyone who asked why she wanted to reach this goal and what benefits she would receive from the goal. Because she had the goal in writing and clearly knew why it was important to her, every time she had a decision to make about money she would stop to think about the impact of that decision on her long-term goal. As a result, she only made decisions that supported her goal of being an independent businesswoman. Within the time Sherrie had expected, she was able to quit her job and start her own business caring for other people's pets.

How Much and How Long to Achieve Your Goals

Now that you've determined financial priorities, the next step is to create a plan for reaching your goals. You've heard it said "Just when I make ends meet they move the ends." Sometimes financial planning can feel the same way, like it's a moving target. To some extent, that's very true. Many factors influence what things cost and their availability when we want them. Inflation, which has run at about 3 percent per year for the past seventy years or so, causes the prices of the things we buy and the services we use to increase regularly (Source: Ibbotson Associates). Supply and demand can also have a similar kind of effect—if everyone in town wants to have their houses repainted at the same time, local painters are able to ask a higher fee than they would otherwise. What does this mean for your planning process? It means that increases in cost for items you're buying are one more thing to take into consideration. In this chapter, we'll help you understand how to do that.

There are a couple of other things to remember here as well. The first is that some things, like cars, are very well made today, and as a result, people are owning them longer than ever before. This effectively reduces the total cost of owning and using these items. And some things are getting cheaper very quickly. Personal computers are a good example of this phenomenon. Today, you can easily set up a home office for under $2,500. Just two years ago, that was not true at all. All of this means that, in order to meet your financial goals, you also have to take into consideration some degree of price unpredictability.

This goal setting stuff has a lot of moving parts, true, but knowing that they are all moving and where they are all going will give you the ability to move with them, and to achieve your goals.

Money and Time

Here's another perspective on how money and time interact. Investment pros talk about the "time value of money." As you intuitively know, the purchasing power of $10.00 today is different from the purchasing power of $10.00 in 1960, 1929, or 1918. From an investment perspective, money you have in your hand today is always worth more than money you expect to have later. Why? Because the purpose of money is to buy things—money you have in hand today can be used to buy good and services, or it can be invested and earn interest that in turn can be used to buy things later on.

Finding the Cost of Your Goals

Now that you have created a solid list of your important financial goals, the next step in the process is to get a handle on the cost of these goals and to develop a step by step process for achieving them.

Take a look at the worksheet on the next page. You may want to make a couple copies of it to use. This worksheet simplifies the goal setting process so that you can take control of it. On the worksheet you are using, fill in the first column, "Your Financial Goals," with the information from the Financial Goal Setting exercise earlier in this chapter.

The next step is to fill in the second column of the worksheet, "The Total Cost of the Goal," with the projected costs, at the time you will actually need the money, of each of your financial goals. You may not currently know the precise figure of a future cost, but you have a good sense for the range, within a few hundred dollars. Just use whatever information you have. If you have no idea at all about the price tag, read ahead. The next few pages of this book will help you gather the information you need for this column of the worksheet. Remember to keep in mind the effects of inflation and any other factors that might affect the prices for your goals. Again, inflation has been quite low over the last several years, approximately 3 percent in most years. Over a long period of time, and on a large amount, however, inflation can add up. Some costs, like medical and college, have increased at a much greater rate than the overall rate of inflation. It's important to look at what the inflation rate has been for your specific goal so you can project what it will be in the future. Consult your local library to get Consumer Price Index (CPI) information, or call a car dealer, or a college of your choice, etc., and ask what the rate of increase has been on an annual basis over the last several years. You'll need to get a calculator and multiply the current cost of the item by the percentage increase you are expecting, for example 6 percent (.06) for a college education. Then you'll need to add the amount that the increase will be for the first year (i.e., assume current cost of college is $20,000 multiplied by .06 equals $1,200 increase for the first year.) The second year cost is now $21,200 ($20,000 plus the $1,200) multiplied by .06, etc., and keep doing this for as many years as you need to save. To calculate the effect of inflation on long-term goals like retirement, try using some of the financial software packages that do this automatically (Quicken or Microsoft Money). Also, many planners and financial services firms have done this research for you.

• • • • •

If your goal is retirement, the next section of the book will help you develop a retirement savings goal customized to your financial situation.

Achieving Financial Goals Worksheet

Today's date is:

1. Your Financial Goals (Retirement, education, house, new car, etc.)	2. The Total Cost of the Goal (If you're not sure of the exact amount, make an educated guess.)	3. Time Frames for Reaching Your Goals (Years from now)	4. The Monthly Savings Amount That Will Get You to Your Goal (From Figure 2.1, Meeting Financial Goals Chart).	5. The Weekly, Bi-Weekly, or Annual Savings Amount That Will Get You to Your Goal (Weekly = box 4 divided by 4, bi-weekly = box 4 divided by 2, annual = box 4 × 12)
Example New Car	$25,000.00	5 years	$340.24	Weekly savings of $85.06

Goals	Cost of Goals	Time Frames	Monthly Savings	Weekly, Biweekly, or Annual Savings

Figure 2.1

Meeting Financial Goals Chart

The (approximate) total dollar cost of your financial goal is:	The number of years you are from your goal right now is: (Shown below is the monthly savings amount that, with an annual 8% return on investment, will enable you to achieve your goal)							
Your Goal Costs	5	10	15	20	25	30	35	40
$1,000.00	$13.61	$5.47	$2.89	$1.70	$1.05	$0.67	$0.44	$0.29
$5,000.00	$68.05	$27.33	$14.45	$8.49	$5.26	$3.35	$2.18	$1.43
$10,000.00	$136.10	$54.66	$28.90	$16.98	$10.51	$6.71	$4.36	$2.86
$25,000.00	$340.24	$136.65	$72.25	$42.44	$26.29	$16.77	$10.90	$7.16
$50,000.00	$680.49	$273.30	$144.49	$84.89	$52.57	$33.55	$21.80	$14.32
$100,000.00	$1,360.97	$546.61	$288.99	$169.77	$105.15	$67.10	$43.59	$28.65
$500,000.00	$6,804.86	$2,733.05	$1,444.93	$848.87	$525.75	$335.49	$217.97	$143.23
$1,000,000.00	$13,609.73	$5,466.09	$2,889.85	$1,697.73	$1,051.50	$670.98	$435.94	$286.45
$1,500,000.00	$20,414.59	$8,199.14	$4,334.78	$2,546.60	$1,577.24	$1,006.47	$653.91	$429.68
$2,000,000.00	$27,219.46	$10,932.19	$5,779.71	$3,395.47	$2,102.99	$1,341.96	$871.88	$572.90

Putting a Price Tag on Your Goals

Homes

Local real estate agents and brokers are the best source of information about current home prices in your area. Ask for a list of houses currently on the market, for information about the size and condition of the homes, and the prices for comparable houses that have sold recently.

College Expenses

The annual *Barron's Profiles of American Colleges* contains up-to-date information on private and public colleges across the country. In addition to all the important data about the school like curriculum and professor backgrounds, it gives prices for tuition and room and board. Schools are listed alphabetically within state or you can reference schools by looking up specific college majors.

Peterson's Guide to Two-Year Colleges provides the same type of information for two-year schools, plus information on financial aid.

Cars

To get an idea of price ranges for cars, consult a copy of *Edmund's Buyer's Decision Guide,* or check their Web site at www.edmunds.com. Edmund's information covers both prices and reviews for new and used foreign and domestic cars, depending on which guide you use. For planning purposes, keep in mind that the invoice price listed is what the dealer pays. The manufacturer's suggested retail price (msrp) is closer to what you would actually pay for the car.

Another good resource for new cars is the *Consumer Reports Car Guide.* The annual April issue of *Consumer Reports* magazine also carries information on car buying. In addition to a review of the vehicles, *Consumer Reports* gives a price range for each vehicle; your price would depend on the options you choose. It's a good idea to know the base cost and the cost of the options so you can be a strong negotiator when you go to purchase your car. This will really put you in the driver's seat!

Retirement: The Granddaddy of Financial Goals

This is certainly the largest financial goal most of us have. Because of the size of the goal and its importance, it requires more planning than all other goals. Many people find the whole idea of planning for retirement daunting: how do you even go after a goal that big? We'll tell you how: one step at a time, one day at a time.

For starters, how big a nest egg do you need to reach your financial goal for retirement? Retirement, unlike things you buy, has a price established by you. Once you've set your goal, you pursue it like any other goal.

This process has three steps:

1. Estimate your retirement budget
2. Estimate your retirement income, given the information you have now
3. Calculate your retirement savings goal

There is no magic to this process; you determine how much you need for your retirement budget. Then figure how much income you can expect to receive from any retirement savings you may already be putting aside for yourself, your pension programs, and Social Security. Your retirement goal is simply the number that will fill the gap between projected income and expenses.

At this point, there is conflicting evidence about the possible demise of the Social Security system. Whether or not you believe you'll receive any benefits from the system, the truth is that the benefits are quite small relative to the cost of maintaining a comfortable lifestyle. Therefore, we encourage you to rely on yourself and the other pensions available to you when it comes to funding a comfortable retirement.

━○← • • • • •

How Big a Nest Egg Do You Need?

Step One: Estimate your retirement budget.
The best way to know what your expenses will be when you retire, an unknown, is to start with what you do know—your current expenses.

Of course, you can expect some of your expenses to change significantly when you retire. Some expenses, like medical costs, are likely to increase, while others, like expenses for professional clothing and entertaining colleagues, will probably drop.

Step Two: Estimate your retirement income, given the information you have now.

There are two different kinds of income you will receive when you retire:

1. Fixed benefits, amounts of income you will receive regularly that you can't change.

2. Income from other assets, like savings and investment accounts.

The list below will help you calculate what you are likely to receive from different places. If you have begun saving and investing for retirement, now is the time to factor that in. Don't worry if you can't fill in all (or even any) of the boxes on the list; the idea here is to investigate the goal so you can fill in the boxes later!

To calculate the amount of income you will receive from personal assets, follow these three steps:

1. Multiply the dollar value of your account balance by the rate of return you are currently earning on that balance. The result is the total annual income you will receive from that one investment. (Example: An account balance of $10,000 earning 8 percent will generate $800 in income annually: $10,000 × .08.) This will give you a rule of thumb number because, of course, the balance will go up when new investment dollars are added.

2. To calculate your monthly income from that investment, take the total annual income from Step 1 and divide it by twelve. In this case, $800 divided by 12 is $66.67; thus the monthly income from this account is almost $67.

3. Finally, just add the totals from both columns to calculate your monthly retirement income.

(continued)

Estimating Your Monthly Retirement Budget Worksheet

Item	Current Monthly Expenses	Estimated Monthly Expenses During Retirement
Housing—mortgage or rent, utilities, and maintenance		
Insurance		
Transportation—car payments, repairs, gas, etc.		
Food—groceries and eating out		
Entertainment and travel		
Personal care—cleaners, drugstore, etc.		
Gifts and donations		
Clothing		
Loan payments		
Medical and dental		
Pet care		
Taxes		
Investments		
Other		
Total		

Income from Investments or Other Assets Worksheet

	Account Value	Rate of Return	Total Annual Income	Monthly Income
Liquid savings (Cash)				
401(k), Other defined contribution plans, etc.				
IRAs				
Investment accounts				
Other assets				
Total				

Income from Fixed Benefits Worksheet

	Monthly Income
Employer's pension plan	
Social Security	
Earned income (such as a part-time job)	
Other	
Total	

Pension benefits. To determine your pension benefits, obtain a benefits statement from each company for which you worked and qualified for pension benefits.

Social Security. Call the Social Security Administration 24 hours a day at 800-772-1213 to hear recorded information or to get a benefit request form. Or, you can visit its Web site at http://www.ssa.gov to get a benefit request form, get an estimate online, or calculate your own retirement benefit.

Time and other income you receive during retirement impact your Social Security benefits. Here are some things to know:

- You can start receiving Social Security benefits at age 62, but they will be at a lower rate than if you wait to retire at age 65 or later.
- You are eligible for cost-of-living increases. These are added to your benefit beginning with the year you reach 62 up to the year you start getting benefits.
- If you delay retirement past age 65—your benefit amount will be increased for every month you are past age 65 but not receiving benefits. These increases are added to your benefit until you reach age 70.
- Up to 85 percent of your Social Security benefit may be taxed if the total of your adjusted gross income, nontaxable interest, and half of Social Security benefit exceeds $34,000 ($44,000 for couples).
- Earning income in retirement will impact your Social Security payments—the penalties that will apply vary by age and the amount of earned income. If you are going to work and receive Social Security benefits, calculate whether you "come out ahead" by earning more than the allocated limit. In some cases, the overall annual income will be more, even if benefits are reduced. In addition, you pay Social Security taxes when you work so the government recalculates your benefits to take into account any extra earnings.

Age	Income Limit	Penalty
62–64	$9,120 (1998 limit) $8,640 (1997 limit)	$1.00 in benefits is withheld for every $2.00 earned over the limit.
65–70	$14,500 (1998 limit) $13,500 (1997 limit)	$1.00 in benefits is withheld for every $3.00 earned over the limit.
70 and older	none	none

Once you are collecting Social Security benefits, income is counted when it is earned—not when it is paid. If income is earned in one year but payment of it is deferred to the following year, it isn't considered earnings for the year you receive it (unless you're self-employed, in which case income counts when you receive it—not when it is earned). The exception would be income paid in a year after you became entitled to Social Security but earned before you became entitled. No non-work income is counted, e.g., investment earnings, annuities, capital gains, pensions, interest, and other government benefits.

The following tables show the impact of earnings on estimated annual Social Security income.

For People under Age 65

If Your Monthly Social Security Benefit Is:	And You Earn:	You Will Receive Yearly Benefits Of:
$400	$8,640 or less	$4,800
$400	$15,000	$1,620
$600	$8,640 or less	$7,200
$600	$15,000	$4,020
$600	$20,000	$1,520
$800	$8,640 or less	$9,600
$800	$15,000	$6,420
$800	$20,000	$3,920

(continued)

For People Ages 65 to 69

If Your Monthly Social Security Benefit Is:	And You Earn:	You Will Receive Yearly Benefits Of:
$400	$13,500 or less	$4,800
$400	$20,000	$2,633
$600	$13,500 or less	$7,200
$600	$20,000	$5,033
$600	$30,000	$1,700
$800	$13,500 or less	$9,600
$800	$20,000	$7,433
$800	$30,000	$4,101

Step Three: Calculate your retirement savings goal.

The third step in the process of establishing a retirement savings goal is to calculate the total dollar amount of the goal. To do this, just take a look at the total income number you just calculated in Step Two, and subtract the expenses you calculated in Step One. If you have a big positive number, great. If, like most people, your estimated income will not cover your expenses, find the amount of the gap, or difference, below and the corresponding total savings goal to the right of it. This is the number you need to enter into column two of the Achieving Financial Goals Worksheet.

Monthly Income Gap	Total Savings Goal
$500.00	$68,141.75
$750.00	$102,212.62
$1,000.00	$136,283.49
$1,500.00	$204,425.24
$1,750.00	$238,496.11
$2,000.00	$272,566.99
$3,000.00	$408,850.48
$5,000.00	$681,417.47
$7,500.00	$1,022,126.21
$10,000.00	$1,362,834.94

Assumptions: This money earns an 8 percent rate of return before taxes are calculated, retirement lasts 30 years, and there is no money left after that 30-year period.

Time can be your friend in the process of achieving financial goals. Often, the goals that benefit the most from the passage of time are those that also take the longest to achieve. Retirement is certainly one of the goals that benefits greatly from the effects of compounding. People often talk about the "magic" of compound interest. Of course, it's not really magic at all. It is, however, a great tool that works for you over time while you are working hard to achieve your goals.

Here's how it works:

- Assume you invest $100 at the beginning of the year.
- This $100 original investment earns interest, say 5 percent compounded annually.
- The $5 in interest is added to your original $100, so at the end of the year you have $105.
- Going into next year, you can earn interest on your $105 investment. The "magic" is that you invest $100 total, but the account earns interest on that investment and the interest. The account will keep growing even if you don't invest more money. (Of course, it will grow more if you do add to it.)

Here's another way to look at our example:

Year 1		Year 2	
Original Investment	$100.00	New Account Balance	$105.00
Plus 5% Interest	$ 5.00	Plus 5% Interest	$ 5.25
New Account Balance	$105.00	Newest Account Balance	$110.25

• • • • •

Set a Time Frame for Achieving Your Goals

Now that you have a handle on the numbers you're actually working with, we'll put them together with your ideal time frames for meeting your goals, and then we'll prioritize them to see when you realistically can accomplish them. Don't worry if everything seems to need to happen at once. This chapter includes budget and money management tools for making more money available to meet your goals. Also, it's important to know that all of these decisions can be reevaluated and realigned whenever they need to be—that's part of the process as well.

At this point, you're ready to consider the issue of time frames—when will you need (or want) the money to achieve the goal you've set for yourself. Some time frames, of course, are established for you, like your children entering college, but most time frames are of your choosing. Even something like when you will retire is your choice—there's no magic to age 65. Remember that you do have the flexibility to change your time frames if you need to. When you reach the goal is something you determine—this gives you great freedom in planning how much money to put away and what kinds of investments to choose.

There are really three variables (things that can be changed) when it comes to setting financial goals:

1. The goal itself (how much of a priority is it, really, and can it be modified in any way?)
2. The time frame for achieving the goal (do you need to buy a house next year, or can you wait for two years instead?)
3. The amount of money that you can save toward achieving your goal (are there other things you can choose to give up in favor of this goal?)

At this point, you want to complete the exercise assuming the "best case" scenario—that you can comfortably achieve all of your goals. If that isn't the case as you look at your household budget, we'll reevaluate the variables (goal, time, and savings amount) to see which one (or ones) has the most wiggle room for you.

Goals That Matter

Later in this chapter you will be using Your Own Ten-Year Plan for Accomplishing Your Goals Worksheet to put your goals in order of their total cost, their time frames, or their importance to you. In a class we taught about investing, we heard this story:

"I completed this worksheet by organizing my goals in order of importance—by which goals mattered most to me. I thought about the fact that a lot of financial goals are based on things that other people think are important, things like having a big house and a fancy car. What's important to me is saving for my retirement, and paying for my daughter's college education, or at least helping her out. I live in an apartment, and I suppose a house would be nice, but being able to travel after I retire really means more to me. So, I put retirement and college at the top of my list, and I took the house off the list. And you know what? It's working. I'm saving and investing just what I planned to."

Try the visioning exercise (where you imagine how it would feel to accomplish all the different goals you have set for yourself) to determine which goals "feel" most important to you.

Go ahead now and take a look at your Achieving Financial Goals Worksheet on page 14, and fill in the time frame block for each goal.

Evaluate and Confirm Financial Priorities

The final step in the process is to figure out what each goal will actually cost you to accomplish, and to make sure that you will be able to accomplish the goals you have set for yourself. Part of the process here is to evaluate the "do-ability" of each goal, in other words, can you reasonably expect to accomplish them given the variables you have assigned (time frame, priority, and available money to set aside), or do you need to reevaluate the variables and make some changes?

Meeting Financial Goals Chart (Figure 2.1) will give you the information you need to fill in the last two columns of the Achieving Financial Goals Worksheet. Find the amount closest to the cost of your goal, when you will actually need the money, then find the number of years from the goal that corresponds to your time frame. Finally, enter the monthly saving amount for the goal in

Column 4 of the worksheet. Use Column 5 of the worksheet to calculate your weekly or annual savings targets.

Before you decide that your goals are too expensive, be sure to read the budgeting information and to complete the budget exercise.

Also, remember that there are two ways to increase the amount of money available to put toward your goals:

1. Increase the amount of money coming in (get a second job, find a way to make a hobby pay, offer a needed service in your community, etc.).
2. Decrease the amount of money going out by reducing current expenses.

Another thing to consider is extending the time frame you have set for the goal. Could you work for a few more years before starting your own business? Could you delay the trip to Hawaii another year to give yourself more time to save for it? The longer the time frame, the less money you need to put away on a regular basis. Before you decide you "can't" meet a goal, change the time frame and see what this does to the amount you need to save. You could also consider a less expensive version of your goal. For example, would a trip to Southern Florida instead of Hawaii be an alternative for you?

Meeting financial goals are gifts to yourself. Time, too, is a gift. Be sure to find the right balance of time and goal—don't make the mistake of being too hard on yourself. All you'll accomplish is to discourage yourself from making further efforts toward reaching your goals.

There is no question that this is the hardest part of the goal-setting process. Most of you know how much money is coming in on an annual, monthly, and/or weekly basis, and you know what your goals are. Finding the money to set aside toward long-term goals is complicated by the number of regular and irregular expenses, as well as by making hard decisions about where to put your "extra" income. But that's why it's called planning.

Setting Up a Regular Savings Plan

Remember this—it is probably one of the most important points in this book: you *must* establish a regular savings and investment plan associated with each of your goals. (We'll cover the investment part later in the book.) If you don't do this, you also don't have any way to attain your goals.

Most of us work for a living and need to make our dreams into reality out of our annual incomes. This is very possible, we're pleased to report, but it does require discipline (yuck!) and making a habit of saving money.

How? There are a number of ways to do this. On payday, write yourself a check for the total amount of your savings goal. If you get paid monthly, set aside the monthly total. If you get paid weekly, set aside the weekly amount. You get the idea.

Most banks, credit unions, and mutual fund companies will take an amount of money you specify directly out of your checking account and move it to a savings or fund account. Frankly, that's the easy part. Deciding to save—and picking the amount to put away—is the more difficult piece of the equation.

The following Your Own Ten-Year Plan for Accomplishing Your Goals Worksheet is a great way to map out your financial goals over a longer period of time. The worksheet is very simple to use. It is set up to track ten years of planning at a time. (If you're feeling very ambitious and would like to take an even longer view, say twenty years, just copy the worksheet and replace the year number 1 with an 11, the 2 with a 12, etc.)

Fill in the name of each of your goals and the amount you will save over the next ten years toward that goal. Taking a long-term perspective lets you see when some goals will be accomplished, which will then let you begin to focus on new goals.

To help you see how this process works, see the Thomas's Ten-Year Plan for Accomplishing Their Goals Worksheet at the end of this chapter. You can see how the Thomas family plans to achieve their goal of saving enough for a down payment on a new car, and once that goal is accomplished, will begin the process of saving a down payment for an addition to their house.

Your Own Ten-Year Plan for Accomplishing Your Goals Worksheet

Goal	Year									
	1	2	3	4	5	6	7	8	9	10
1.										
2.										
3.										
4.										
5.										
6.										
7.										
8.										
9.										
10.										
Total										

The Thomas's Ten-Year Plan for Accomplishing Their Goals

Mike and Cathy Thomas, both 32, with two kids, ages four and one

Goal	Year 1	2	3	4	5	6	7	8	9	10
1. College	$2,000	$2,000	$2,000	$2,000	$2,000	$2,000	$2,000	$2,000	$2,000	$2,000
2. Retirement	$2,500	$2,500	$2,500	$2,500	$2,500	$2,500	$2,500	$2,500	$2,500	$2,500
3. Down payment on a new car	$1,500	$1,500								
4. Down payment on addition to house			$1,500	$1,500	$1,500					
5. Travel fund						$1,500	$1,500	$1,500	$1,500	$1,500
6.										
7.										
8.										
9.										
10.										
Total	$6,000	$6,000	$6,000	$6,000	$6,000	$6,000	$6,000	$6,000	$6,000	$6,000

Evaluate and Confirm Your Personal Financial Priorities

So What's the Big Deal with All This Planning, Anyway?

You may be wondering at this point why we've focused so much on thoughtful planning for meeting financial goals. The reason is simple, and a lesson you've probably learned already. For most people, the immediate—a fun, nice dinner with friends, for example—is more appealing and screams louder for attention than stodgy and longer-term goals like retirement. For many of us, the focus is on instant gratification. Which is not to say that we don't recognize the importance of long-term goals, but we often feel that goals like college and retirement are too big to tackle, so we simply ignore them.

We're here to tell you that the goals you can imagine in some ways to be real and the goals that match your values are exactly the things you can accomplish. The goals you have set using the process outlined in this book are important and meaningful to you, and you know exactly what you need to do to achieve them. These are the goals you will accomplish.

In the short term, it's important to learn to develop the ability to pause before spending money and ask yourself—is this thing I am about to buy really more important than saving this amount toward a longer-term goal? If controlling spending that way seems like it will be too hard, try simply writing a check to your savings account as if it's one of your fixed expenses. That way, whatever is left can be spent on whatever you have budgeted to buy.

The Pleasure/Pain Principle

Spending money is fun, don't you think? Buying new things, going new places, trying new restaurants, or just frequenting a favorite restaurant. But it all adds up. And it can add up to putting off long-term goals that are just as— if not more—important. Saving money, for most of us anyway, isn't really "fun."

But we'd like to share a real thrill with you. After a couple of years of regular savings toward a goal, an account balance starts to build up. If you've picked investments other than a savings account for your money, which you may want to do depending on the nature of the goal, you should start to see some real growth. Opening that account statement in the mail or calling a toll-free number to find out how your account balance has grown is absolutely, hands down, one of the best feelings ever.

The very last step in the goal-setting process, now that your goals have been identified, written down, and prioritized with time and savings amounts attached, is to anticipate enjoying the feeling that will come from reaching those goals. Know that, at this point, you have already done a lot of hard work; thinking about all of this stuff is hard and complicated. Achieving financial goals is not simply a matter of money, it's a matter of mind *and* money.

The "Good News" Approach to Budgeting

Budgeting—keeping track of your money—is just as important as goal setting. They are complementary processes. Conscious budgeting is, for most of us, the only way to make money available for our longer-term financial goals.

We are firm believers in the devil-you-know theory; it's always better to know exactly what you're dealing with when it comes to budgeting, even if the news feels kind of grim at first. To be able to make decisions about changing your approach to spending, in order to make more money available for financial goals, you need to know where the money is going in the first place.

Where Your Money Goes Now

Money is hard to keep track of. Three dollars go for coffee and a danish, two dollars in quarters for the parking meter, and another five dollars for lunch with the gang from the office. And ATMs don't help, either. We take money out of the ATM and spend it, and then sometimes before we even record the withdrawal, we've gone back for more! Most of us don't know where all of our money goes. How could we? Sure, we know the big bills, rent or mortgage, utilities, car payments, loan payments, etc., but most of us don't keep detailed records of all of the smaller expenses—which have an ugly habit of adding up over time.

Beth and Tom serve as an example They told us they were so excited to get their new software program to track their expenses on their home computer. They selected categories for each expense but when something didn't fit neatly into a category, they tagged it "miscellaneous." Miscellaneous items covered their many ATM withdrawals and the many ongoing payments on their credit card bills. At the end of the year, when completing their taxes, they pulled totals for all categories off their software program. The miscellaneous category was a grand total of $3,500! They looked at this large number and couldn't even begin to determine where it had all been spent. They vowed to track every dollar more closely next year. $3,500 would have been a great contribution to long-term savings goals, or a nice trip, or a down payment on a car, or any other desirable large expense.

The goal of The Good News Budget Worksheet later in this chapter is to support you in the process of reaching your financial goals by taking a close look at where your money goes now. This worksheet will take you through the budgeting process.

When you look under expenses on the budget worksheet, you'll notice that we started with savings and investments before alphabetizing the list. We did that deliberately. Because the goal of this book is to help you make comfortable and sound investing decisions, it makes sense to start the budgeting process by planning to meet your financial goals.

Before you start using the budget worksheet, make several copies. You'll want to come back to this exercise over time, as your goals and financial situation change. Take a few minutes to fill it out for the most recent full month.

If you know what all the numbers are off the top of your head, great. If not, go ahead and do the research on your old bills and checkbook and see what your expenses are for each of these categories. Another way to do this is to track your expenses (down to the penny) for a month and to complete the worksheet.

OK. So now you know how the budget looks. If you have more expenses than money, and if adding in the savings and investing number only makes things worse, don't worry. (We say this a lot. Why? Because worrying doesn't add to your bank balance. Taking steps to change your long-term financial situation, on the other hand, does.) Make sure (and this is very important) that you can fit all of the fixed expenses (rent, car payments, and other stuff you have no ability to change), the variable expenses that matter the most to you, and your savings and investing amount for long-term goals, in the same budget. If the numbers don't fit, start with another copy of the budget worksheet, and keep making changes in each category until income and expenses match.

There is no science to this, and no financial expert can tell you which things matter the most to you and your family. The only way to make the choices that need to be made is to prioritize them. Remember the exercise we did earlier to help you imagine your goals being real? This same tool can be helpful in choosing budget priorities, too.

If the numbers work, great! You're on your way. If they don't, you'll need to go back to the goal-setting process and revisit the other two variables for each of your goals (the goal itself and the time frame for the goal), and see what changes can be made that decrease the amount of money you need to save each pay period. Another reason for doing this, besides simply giving you the tools to achieve your goals, is to empower you to make comfortable decisions about the things that mean the most to you and how to go about getting to where you want to be.

Once you have identified your financial goals, you can save money toward them. You may have actually started this saving process already for some of your goals. Depending on the time frame for your goals and how much money you want to accumulate over time, you'll probably want to also invest some of the money you've saved. The rest of this book focuses on making appropriate, profitable and most importantly, comfortable investing decisions for yourself.

The Good News Budget Worksheet

(Now you'll know where your money's going!)

Monthly Income—Money In

Take-home pay (all sources, including part-time)   _____

Dividend/interest income (after-tax)   _____

Pension/disability/Social Security   _____

Other sources (alimony, hobbies, etc.)   _____

Total Income (100%)   _____

Monthly Expenses—Money Out

Savings and investments   _____

Charitable contributions   _____

Child care   _____

Clothing   _____

Credit card payments   _____

Eating out   _____

Education   _____

Food and beverages (groceries and liquor)   _____

Fun and entertainment   _____

Gifts   _____

Home maintenance and improvements   _____

Insurance (health, life, disability)   _____

Investment expenses and fees   _____

Medical care (not included in insurance)   _____

Mortgage or rent payments   _____

Personal care (dry cleaners, drugstore, etc.)   _____

Personal property insurance (home, car, etc.)   _____

Pet care (food and veterinarian)   _____

Property taxes (home, car, etc.)   _____

Public transportation/commuting expenses   _____

Telephone (include cell phones and long distance)   _____

Utilities (heat, light, water, sewer, cable)   _____

Vehicle maintenance and fuel   _____

Vehicle payments   _____

Total (100%)   _____

The Difference (Income less Expenses) $_____

The Debt Challenge

Debt is the beast many of us hide—even from ourselves. If credit card debt, too many loans to buy more stuff, or a period of financial hardship have caused bills to pile up, here's a process to figure your way out. The reason for figuring a way out is simple: owing money means you don't really own all of what you earn. You can't use all of what is leftover after paying your current expenses to invest or to buy other things you need. This table will help you do the math and to keep track of what you're paying and what you still owe.

The first step is to add up what you owe. All of it. Then, looking at the total debt amount and your household budget, decide how much you can reasonably afford to pay off each month. You'll need to communicate with each of your creditors and confirm that they are willing to accept the payment that you can afford to give them. It's important to get in touch with your creditors directly and be frank about your situation. Most creditors are willing to work with you if they find you are making a concerted effort to pay the debt over time. Once you've gained agreement from creditors about the amount you will pay, you know how much needs to go toward paying down the debts.

Interest rates on debt will mean that the balance you're looking at today will not be the total amount paid over time. In fact, interest rates can be so high on things like credit cards that if you don't pay enough each month on your balance, the interest accumulating means that next month you owe even more without even buying any additional items! First, find out what the interest rate is on each piece of debt. Next, prioritize the debt to be paid in order of highest interest rate first, and lowest interest rate last. The creditors charging you the highest rates of interest should be paid first because paying interest is contributing to the creditors' ability to build wealth, not yours! To figure your monthly amount, including interest, take the balance you owe and multiply it by the interest rate charged (i.e., $1,500 to the furniture store at 18 percent (0.18) interest equals $270 in interest) and add this to your total current amount. The total debt amount is now $1,770 at the end of the year, if you made no payments. As you pay off the balance, the interest impact will go down. It can be a complicated process to figure out exact amounts taking interest into consideration as you continue to pay down your debt because for each month you also are paying interest on the interest charged in the previous months. This exercise is meant to help you look at your total debt and figure out a simple way to begin to pay it off—so you can find some money to invest to begin to build your wealth. If you have a great deal of debt with many different interest rates and a long-term payoff process, it might make sense to take an adult education course on managing money to learn more about budgeting to pay off debt. You also may try to pay off some high-interest debts with a lower-interest loan.

For purposes of this exercise, let's be fairly simplistic and take the debt amount, with the annual interest amount added, as your total debt owed. Now for each account on which you owe money, fill in the name and the balance on the following List of Debts Worksheet. If you're having problems with this assignment, skip ahead to the Calvert List of Debts Chart for an example.

Mike and Ellen Calvert have a number of bills with balances total of $5,300 and a total of $6,000 after factoring in interest. They feel they can reasonably pay around $450 per month toward their debt, as they would like to be out of debt in 12 months. Their creditors have agreed to the payment schedule outlined here. They allocate their monthly debt repayment evenly among their bills. If one of the debts had a particularly high interest rate, we would recommend paying off one debt earlier by increasing the amount of that payment, and reducing the others, but still paying the monthly budget amount.

The huge benefit to this simple approach is that it makes a big number, like $6,000, very manageable to pay off.

Too Many Goals—Not Enough Money

Once you've gotten a handle on your goals, budget, and debt (or lack of it) you can make real, substantial progress toward your larger financial goals. But what if you completed this section, charted goals, developed a budget and debt repayment approach, and have nothing left over with which to build wealth? Don't panic, there are some options for finding money. The key is to know what your priorities are and stay focused on them. If you really want to build wealth and make smart financial decisions, you may have to give up some day-to-day niceties so there's money left over for longer term gain.

First, keep the list of goals clearly posted wherever you'll be sure to see them on a daily basis. If your goals are visible and memorable, it will be eas-

List of Debts Worksheet

Debts Owed to Others

Account	Balance x Interest Rate	Monthly Payment Schedule											
		1	2	3	4	5	6	7	8	9	10	11	12
Total													
Debt Remaining													

Calvert List of Debts Chart

| Debts Owed to Others | | Monthly Payment Schedule | | | | | | | | | | | |
Account	Balance x Interest Rate	1	2	3	4	5	6	7	8	9	10	11	12
Furniture store	$1,500 at 18% interest **$1,770**	$111											
Ellen's credit card	$800 at 15% interest **$920**	$111											
Mike's credit card	$500 at 12% interest **$560**	$111											
Car loan	$2,500 at 10% interest **$2,750**	$111											
Total	**$6,000**	$444	$444	$444	$444	$444	$444	$444	$444	$444	$444	$444	$444
Debt Remaining		$5,556											

ier to give up that dinner out, or expensive "must have" shirt and, instead, put the money aside for saving and investing. It helps to be reminded of much desired future goals when feeling "deprived" of something we want today.

Next, review the budget. If there were surprises or questions about inflows and outflows, chart every expense for the next one to two months. Keep track of everything—get a receipt even for a cup of coffee because little expenses add up. If you know where the money is actually going, it's easier to find ways to cut back or eliminate expenses. One couple we know found they were spending close to $8,000 a year on dinners out. They both worked and ate out about three times a week for an average cost of $50. Once they realized how much money dining out was costing, they immediately shifted the money into an investment account and made nice dinners at home instead, sharing the grocery shopping, cooking, and cleanup chores.

Next, consider other ways to add to income sources. Could you take a second job for a period of time, or start a new—more profitable—career? Do you have a talent that could be sold—maybe a hobby or other area of expertise? We know a woman who loved to dance and became quite good at it. She turned her love of dancing into a second job by offering ballroom dancing lessons at night and on weekends. She contributed all of the money she made to her investment account.

Is there someone else you know who might benefit from the goals you've set? Is there a way to combine goals with another person so that more than one person is saving toward the same goal over time? Maybe a friend of yours would also like to go to Hawaii and could contribute to a joint account. The cost of airfare would be individual, but a hotel room, car rental, and sightseeing events might all be shared expenses. The one account established for Hawaii would grow much faster if two people were contributing together. It can also be fun to share a goal with someone else—and share the contributions to the savings account, too.

Look for "hidden" places where you may have money in small sums that you haven't thought of using for investing, like gifts of cash at birthdays and holidays or loose change thrown into a piggy bank. Find ways to do things less expensively, like taking public transportation instead of paying for parking, or renewing your library card instead of buying books at the bookstore. When you do pay off a loan or credit card, continue "paying" the same amount of money every month but into an investment account. Don't be afraid that you don't have enough money to get started investing: some mutual funds will let you begin investing with as little as $25 if you agree to make regular contributions. We'll talk about investing in mutual funds in Chapter 17. After you've identified your goals, getting started putting some money away is the most important next step toward building wealth.

PART

2

Understanding Risk

In the investment world, risk is a very important concept. Now, before you say to yourself, "I know all about risk, I know what it means, and I know how it feels to take risks," we'd like to point out that risk as you view it, and risk as investment pros view it, are probably not the same thing. This section will address two different approaches to risk—the investment professionals' approach and your personal approach—and the impact of both views of risk on investment decision making.

You might know that investments are evaluated and labeled according to the level of risk they are deemed to have. Risk "levels" also can be assigned to people, goals, and investment approaches. You may think of bungee jumping as personally risky, and it can be. Investment pros see "credit and interest rates" as risky, and they can be, from an investment perspective. Personal approaches to risk, our individual "risk levels," so to speak, and assessments of risk from an investment perspective can be two quite different things. In order to understand the risk labels assigned to different investments by investment pros, you must understand how the investment world defines risk. And in order to apply it to your own personal situation, you need to know how you feel about taking risks. The next few chapters will help you to do both of these things.

The trick to making investment decisions that are both profitable and comfortable for you is to find investments that make sense to you in terms of your own perspective about risk taking, as well as from an investment risk perspective.

Evaluate How You Feel about Taking Risks

For most of us, risk is a "trigger" word, meaning that it provokes a reaction or response. The idea of taking risks may get your adrenaline going because you feel adventurous and confident, or because it frightens you. Although you will have your own response to risk taking, it is important to understand how risk is used in the context of making investment decisions. Risk, when applied to investments, can be looked at as simply a descriptive label to help an investor see where each investment falls in relation to another on the spectrum of measurement that we call, "risk."

The word *risk* is an emotion-laden word. Most of us think of ourselves as either "risk takers" or as "risk avoiders," and some of us fall somewhere in between in terms of our comfort with risk. Most of us apply our feelings about risk fairly consistently, meaning that we make the same kind of judgments about risk regardless of the kind of risk we're taking at that particular moment. Certainly some of us are risk takers in some parts of our lives (i.e., speaking in public, challenging traditions) and risk avoiders in others (i.e., parachuting out of an airplane, riding in a rodeo). In general, though, we all operate with behaviors that are fairly consistent and can quickly identify ourselves as comfortable with risk taking, or not.

Fortunately, or unfortunately, depending on your approach, risk is unavoidable when making investment decisions. Without assuming some level of risk in investing, you are unlikely to reach all of your financial goals. Very "safe" investments probably will not earn enough interest to keep even with in-flation—much less contribute to wealthbuilding. On the other hand, not in-vesting is in and of itself a risk—the risk of lost opportunity, or of not making enough money to reach your goals.

Before making the leap of applying your personal risk-taking perspective to investment decision making, it is important first to understand your feelings about risk. This exercise will help you do that.

Taking Personal Risks

The goal of this exercise is to help you develop a sense of your own comfort with risk taking in general, and to evaluate some of the risks you have taken to achieve certain results. Once you have an understanding of your comfort with risk taking, you will have developed a framework for thinking about your personal approach to risk. Then you can begin to evaluate actual invest-ments within the framework of your personal preferences, rather than just on the basis of their investment risks.

To begin, using the Risk-Taking Worksheet below to make a list in the first column of some of the important risks you've taken in your life. For purposes of this exercise, forget you are reading a book on investment decision making. Just list risks in general and don't try to capture every one, just those that felt like the biggest or hardest when you took them. Feel free to in-clude investment choices you have made, but also include other kinds of risks you have taken, like career changes, trips to new places, etc. In the next column, write the goal you were hoping to achieve when you took each risk.

Be sure to list the risks that resulted in accomplishments, too. As we look back at our lives, we have a very human tendency to reframe the risks. Our 20/20 hindsight can make them seem less like real risks and more like really good planning. After all, we brag about the size of the fish we catch, too, and that's OK. Just be sure to recognize the risks for what they were at the time you took them so that you get an accurate picture of who you are as a risk taker. As you complete the list, focus on decisions that represented real choice points for you, where one choice meant taking a risk, and the other didn't. If you have more risks that you'd like to consider than will fit in the spaces, continue the exercise onto another piece of paper.

Now, take a minute to reflect on each risk you listed. Try to remember how you felt when you took the risk. Did you have a physical reaction to what you were doing? Were you scared, thrilled, or confident? Write down in the worksheet's third column a quick note about how you felt.

Finally, in the fourth column, write down the actual outcome of the situation. Did you get what you wanted? Or did it turn out to be one of those "it seemed like a good idea at the time" kinds of things? Be sure to include the risks you took that turned out to be "learning experiences." As frustrating as those can be when they happen, they are useful to us over time. Often we learn more from what we see as our failures than we do from our successes.

Take a minute to look at your worksheet. Which of the risks you took are most closely linked to your values? Many people are more willing to take risks to accomplish the things they value most. Looking at your list, do you see any patterns about the kinds of risks you are comfortable taking or the kinds of goals you are comfortable taking risks to accomplish? Make some notes about the kinds of risks you've taken in the space for notes at the bottom of your worksheet.

• • • • •

Risk-Taking Worksheet

Risk	Goal	How You Felt	Final Outcome
Quit corporate job—with its stable income and benefits package	To start a home-based business and spend more time with family	Unsure and worried about future earnings and scared about losing consistent paycheck	Home-based business is providing a nice income, spending more time with family

Notes:

_____

_____

_____

_____

_____

A Personal Story about Risk

A young man we met recently told us this story about taking risks. Joe Marcus had been working for a large company for many years. Joe had a good job with excellent pay and benefits that his family relied on. He and his wife Elaine had recently had their first baby. His work situation troubled him a lot—he'd been asked by his superiors to do things that were, in his opinion, very bad ideas and perhaps even unethical. The last straw came when Joe's boss asked him to do something Joe felt was completely unethical. Joe asked for time to think about the request. After talking it over with his wife, Joe quit his job the next day.

Now, for most of us, quitting a good job sounds very risky. And there certainly were risks associated with his decision. But for Joe, being in a work environment like the one he was in felt like a bigger risk. Joe valued his integrity far more than he valued his paycheck, and felt comfortable that he could find another job or begin to follow his dream of working for himself.

Joe's story illustrates how relative risk is—what feels like a risk to you or me simply doesn't look the same to someone else. Also, over time our perceptions of risk change. What feels risky at one point in our lives may feel more or less so later on as circumstances change.

How Other People Assess Your Comfort with Investment Risk

Aside from knowing yourself a little bit better and being able to make more comfortable decisions, there is another very practical reason for assessing your personal risk-taking comfort in the context of investment decision making. Most investment firms, and many investment advisers, currently use what are called in the industry "risk profiles" or "risk questionnaires." You'll either fill out a form or answer a list of questions the firm has created. The questions are designed to give the person quizzing you an assessment of your level of comfort with investment risk, rather than your feelings about risk taking in general. Once the results of the "quiz" are tallied, the investment firm or adviser uses the information to make investment recommendations.

All of that is just fine, assuming the questionnaire is sound—and the quality of these tools varies widely, of course—and the person making the judgment call about which investment(s) to recommend to you really understands how to use the tool.

Once you have assessed your comfort level with personal and investment risk yourself, as you have done throughout this chapter, you'll know better how to respond to a risk questionnaire. And most importantly, you can evaluate if the results of a risk questionnaire that someone else gives you are on the mark or off base.

Investment Risk

The whole discussion of risk changes dramatically when we place it in the context of investments. For the most part, in the investment world, the risks of investing are described in rather flat, unemotional terms, despite the fact that the words are very powerful. Of course, other types of businesses categorize their products, too. The gasoline business, for example. They use words like leaded, unleaded, diesel, premium, or regular to describe different levels of quality and different types of products. The investment business is not any different in its efforts to categorize its investment products.

At the same time, risk, for most people, can have a very negative feeling. Risk means doing something you're uncomfortable with, learning to do something new, making a leap of faith—all things to which you may have an emotional reaction. Unleaded, on the other hand, is simply a type of gasoline you're buying. Either the gas has lead in it or it doesn't. Your car either takes regular or premium. It's hard to have feelings about gas, unleaded or otherwise, which makes applying labels about kinds of gas simple. Applying the labels of risk to investing, because it involves the use of a powerful word and concept—risk—is a bit more complicated.

We're not suggesting that categorizing investments according to risk levels is a bad idea. We are suggesting that there are many different kinds of risks related to investments and many different ways of evaluating those risks. Investors need to be aware of all of these. And even though you won't find many investment professionals talking about it, there are also lots of feelings associated with taking investment risks. We'll talk more about this connection later on in Chapter 8. First, let's focus on the meaning of risk that most investment experts use.

Let's start by categorizing investments according to risk levels, just as the investment business does. For the most part, investment experts link the idea of investment risk to the idea of change in the value of the investment. This is generally defined by two factors:

1. The volatility of an investment—how much its returns go up and down. A bank certificate of deposit (CD) has very little volatility (another word for that is fluctuation), while aggressive stock funds generally experience much more volatility over time. Therefore, on a risk scale, the CD would be at the low risk end of the spectrum while the aggressive stock fund would be at the high end.

2. The safety of your principal—the money you originally invested. To come back to our example, a bank CD is generally very safe; most are insured by the FDIC (Federal Deposit Insurance Corporation), which guarantees the safety of bank deposits up to $100,000. On the other hand, an aggressive stock is not very "safe" according to this definition, because you could, in certain circumstances lose the entire amount of your original investment.

The Investment Roller Coaster

October 19, 1987, is called "Black Monday" in the securities and investment business. That's because the Dow Jones Industrial Average (DJIA) dropped more than 500 points (about 23 percent of the market's value) in one day. Sounds pretty risky if you had a lot of money in the market, right?

Investors who simply sat tight were rewarded with a market that rebounded slightly by year end. For most people, that translated to a "flat" year, more or less. Investors who sold into the slide locked in their losses. Investors who went shopping saw their stocks grow dramatically over the next few years. Now, with that famous 20/20 hindsight, the situation doesn't seem to have been quite so risky after all. As you can see, the risks we consider in investing, and our perceptions of them, can change a lot at different points in time.

Late in 1997, we experienced similar plunges in the Dow—and equally speedy recoveries. This time, many so called "little" investors rode out the roller coaster ride. Many pros responded by either dumping stocks or going shopping for bargains. All of this activity just confirms the importance of staying calm during the storm, taking a long-term view of investing, and holding the money you needed in the short term in something other than stocks.

There are lots of other risk factors, besides the standard ones used to categorize investments, to consider within your investment decision-making framework, and they include things like:

- Not investing to begin with
- Not earning enough on your investments to reach your goals
- Not fully understanding investments you have chosen
- Not diversifying your investments enough
- Choosing investments that perform poorly
- Not having enough information to fully understand or follow the behavior of the investment
- Not feeling comfortable asking for help

You may have other things you want to add to this list. Go ahead and create your own list of risks related to investing from the experiences you've had, or factors you want to consider.

Risk and Return

The investment industry typically evaluates individual investments based on risk, as we've talked about, and on another critically important factor: the return the investment can generate. These two factors are always present in an investment, and how they interact impacts how much your money can grow. The general rule is that investors are rewarded for taking on risk, and the reward comes in the form of return on investment. As a result, investments with less risk generally offer less return, and investments that offer more return are generally riskier. Investment experts call this consideration the risk/reward trade-off. As you plan your approach to wealthbuilding, you can choose which one is most important to you at any point, and you can pick investments and combinations of investments that you feel comfortable with.

When you select investments, you need to think about how much return you want to earn, and how much investment risk you are comfortable taking to achieve the return. In general, the very "best" investments are those that have the least risk and offer the most return. The "worst" investments, as you can probably guess by now, are those that have the highest levels of risk and offer the lowest returns.

This chart in Figure 5.1 is often used to illustrate this idea. It shows the balance of risk and return for the three types of investments you hear about most often: the three core asset classes of cash, bonds, and stocks. We'll talk in detail about these different types of investments in Part 3 of this book, Building Your Portfolio. As you can see, the investments that take on the most risk also offer the most potential return. The opposite is also true. Cash investments take the least risk and offer the least return. Bonds take on more risk and offer more return than cash. Stocks take on the highest level of risk of the three core asset classes, and offer the most potential return over time.

Sometimes, rather than this risk and return chart, you'll see something that looks like a thermometer, or a bar. Whatever it looks like, risk and return charts are all designed to express the same idea.

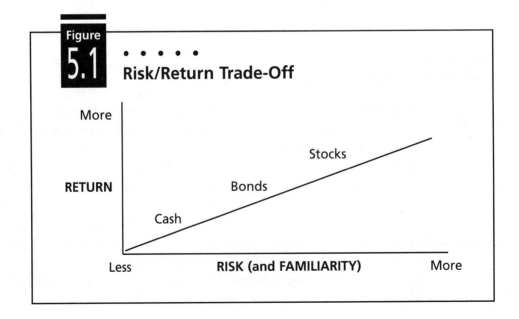

Figure 5.1 • • • • •
Risk/Return Trade-Off

In our conversations with investors, we've observed something interesting about this chart. People are for the most part, very familiar with cash investments, less familiar with bonds, and are generally least familiar with stocks. So if you replace the word "risk" at the bottom of the figure with the word "familiarity," the chart is equally accurate.

Defining Investment Risk

It may seem as if we've said all there is to say about the risks of investing. Not so. Investment risk, as we've said, is a term that describes the possibility of two things happening. The first is the volatility—fluctuation—of investment returns or earnings. The second is the possibility of losing the principal you invested to begin with.

But what creates these two kinds of risks? A number of things. Are there other kinds of risks related to investing that are also worth considering? Absolutely. The truth of the matter is that even people in the investment business have had a hard time agreeing on how to define and communicate all of the different kinds of risks related to investing.

Next we'll talk about a number of different kinds of investing risks. This is where we start to see an interaction between the investment definitions of risk and your personal thoughts or feelings about risk. As you read through this information, think about your own personal perspective on each of these risks. Perhaps you don't agree that one or another of the risks on the list is particularly significant to your own situation. That's your decision to make. The important information here is to understand what these different types of risks are, their technical definitions, so to speak, and how you feel about each of them.

We've included in this list some nontraditional definitions of risk, too, to give you a frame of reference for some other factors that affect investment decision making.

The Concept of Risk

When you invest money, you are giving someone else the opportunity to use your money however they choose. In return, they pay you for the opportunity to use your money. How much you earn by giving someone this opportunity depends on their ability to make good choices about how to use your money. If you are making a direct investment in a stock or a bond, how much you are paid for the use of your money generally depends on how much risk there is in returning your money to you. If there is little doubt that your money will be returned, you will be paid—in relative terms—very little. If the risk of your money not being returned is high, you will certainly want to be compensated for taking that risk.

Figures 5.2 and 5.3 give you an idea of how much investments in cash, stocks, and bonds have paid people over a very long period of time. When

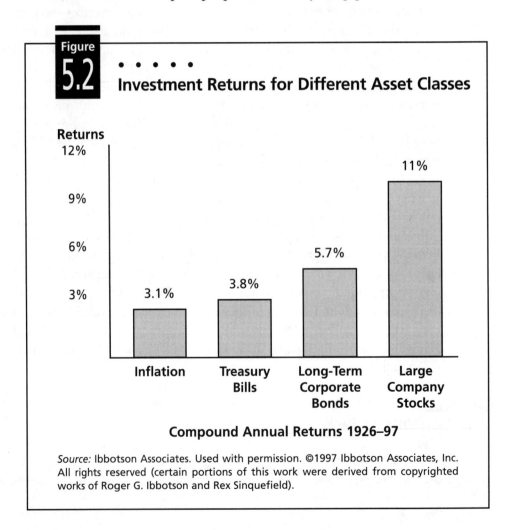

Figure 5.2

• • • • •
Investment Returns for Different Asset Classes

Returns

- 11% — Large Company Stocks
- 5.7% — Long-Term Corporate Bonds
- 3.8% — Treasury Bills
- 3.1% — Inflation

Compound Annual Returns 1926–97

Source: Ibbotson Associates. Used with permission. ©1997 Ibbotson Associates, Inc. All rights reserved (certain portions of this work were derived from copyrighted works of Roger G. Ibbotson and Rex Sinquefield).

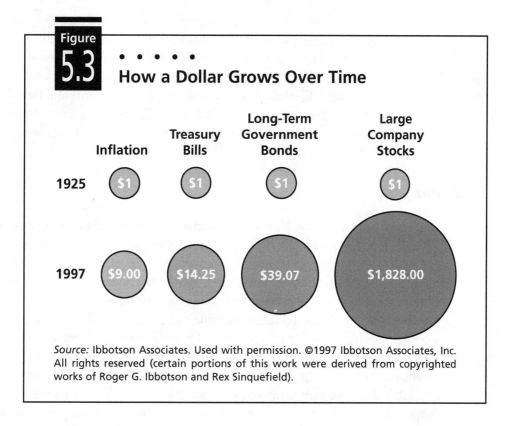

Figure 5.3

• • • • •

How a Dollar Grows Over Time

	Inflation	Treasury Bills	Long-Term Government Bonds	Large Company Stocks
1925	$1	$1	$1	$1
1997	$9.00	$14.25	$39.07	$1,828.00

Source: Ibbotson Associates. Used with permission. ©1997 Ibbotson Associates, Inc. All rights reserved (certain portions of this work were derived from copyrighted works of Roger G. Ibbotson and Rex Sinquefield).

looking at the numbers, keep in mind that stocks are considered to be the most risky and Treasury bills the least risky of the three investment types.

Different Kinds of Investment Risk

Accumulation Risk

This is simply the risk that you might not accumulate all of the money you need to reach a particular investment goal in the time that you need it.

Business Risk

All businesses have cycles. Some cycles are very good and business is great, and sometimes the opposite is true. Circumstances can change very quickly for businesses, weakening companies that seemed so solid weeks or months earlier. A good example of a business cycle is the opening of a new mall. At first, lots of people come to the mall and buy things because it's new and they are curious. Over time, the mall gets old and run down, and the stores in it don't do so well. Cycles happen at different times for different businesses, and can be bad—or good—for the value of an investment. The best way to manage this kind of risk is to be sure that the investments you choose are from different kinds of businesses.

Credit Risk

This is the risk that a person, business, or government that has borrowed your money will not be able to return it to you or pay you for the use of it as it has promised. There can be different reasons for this: a talented home builder might also be a terrible business manager, unable to manage cash flow effectively. This would mean that the contractor might have a hard time coming up with loan interest payments and return of principal. A business like this contractor's would be described as a "bad credit risk." On the other hand, a person or business who manages cash flow effectively and is able to pay bills and loans off quickly can be described as a "good credit risk." Your own credit risk has probably been evaluated if you've ever applied for a credit card or a loan of any kind. If a bank thinks you're likely to repay the loan on time, you'll get the credit you've applied for, and you might even be able to negotiate a better interest rate.

Inflation Risk

Most things cost more today than they used to. Inflation risk is the risk that things will keep getting more expensive. Because there is no sign that this risk is going away, it is important to choose investments that will grow faster than the rate at which things get more expensive, the rate of inflation.

Interest Rate Risk

Interest rates are the rates banks and other lenders charge to borrow money. The prime rate is the rate of interest the most creditworthy businesses are charged for the money they borrow. Interest rates can change for a number of reasons. The Federal Reserve Bank (the "Fed") is responsible for managing the relationship between inflation and interest rates. If inflation is high—things are getting more expensive very quickly—the Fed might raise interest rates. They would make it harder, by making it more expensive, to borrow money to buy things. If spending slows down, stores will cut prices in an effort to sell their merchandise. And inflation with fall. Or so the theory goes.

From an investment perspective, interest rate risk is the risk that a change in interest rates will decrease the value of an investment. This applies primarily to bonds or other types of investments that also pay interest, but stocks are also affected by changes in interest rates. Interest rates influence how much it costs companies to run their businesses. Like most people, most businesses have to borrow money in order to be able to do all the things they want and need to do to grow themselves. As interest rates go up, the costs of borrowing do too, causing businesses to take money they might have paid out to investors as earnings and to use it to keep current on their debt.

Because bonds pay interest, their prices—how much it costs to buy them—are affected by the rates of interest other investments are paying. If you are being paid 5 percent interest on your bond, and current interest rates being paid on other investments are higher than that, your 5 percent bond is an undesireable investment and its seing price will drop. If interest rates are lower than 5 percent, your bond will be a more valuable investment, and its price will go up.

Market Risk

The word "market" describes a place where things of a similar type are bought and sold. Farmers' markets sell fruit, vegetables, and other farm products. Stock markets sell stocks, and bond markets sell bonds. Market risk is the risk that the entire market for the type of investment you have chosen will suffer a decline. In other words, many similar types of stocks, or many similar types of bonds, or even all stocks and all bonds may move in the same direction at the same time. Of course, if things are moving up, you benefit. If the market moves down, however, you might find your investment results disappointing. You absolutely cannot avoid this risk. You can help to make it less of an issue by investing in several different investment markets at the same time. That way, when the market for one type of investment isn't so good, the market for another type of investment may very well be better. The chances are good that if you have a few different types of investments that are sold in different markets, somewhere in the market your money will be performing well for you! This strategy is called *diversification.*

Opportunity Risk (or "Cost")

Because most of us have only a certain amount of money to invest at any point in time, when we choose an investment, we are at the same time choosing not to use our money for something else. Opportunity risk is the risk that another, better investment opportunity will come along and you will not have money available to take advantage of it. Making choices that you are confident about will help you feel comfortable rather than regretful. But opportunity risk is completely unavoidable. It's like the risk of not picking the absolutely best ice cream flavor every time you eat ice cream!

Trust and Control

If you seek investment advice or invest in mutual funds, as so many people do, trust and control are important issues to think about. You need, as a consumer, to trust the professionals you are hiring to manage your money and advise you about investments and investment decision making. Many people have told us they are reluctant to ask questions of their investment advisers or push for answers they can understand. People have told us they don't know what professional licenses their advisers have, or even why they are qualified to deliver investment advice. You have a right to feel that your advisers have your best interests at heart. It is also in their best interests to know that you understand how your money is being managed. At a practical level, keep asking questions until you know what you feel you need to. Someone who doesn't want to answer questions shouldn't have your business anyway.

The same goes for the people who manage mutual funds. Today, most people choose to invest in mutual funds, managed by an investment professional. This professional chooses the individual investments in the fund and pools your money, along with that of others, to buy them. You will have the opportunity to read reports about how your investments are doing, but you probably won't ever meet the portfolio manager or team. You will have to trust that they are qualified to manage your money, and be comfortable that they have day-to-day control over it. So be sure to ask all the questions you need to to feel comfortable with your choices.

As we've said, it's important to think about both your personal approach to risk taking and the investment business approach to risk at the same time. The Risk Worksheet gives you the chance to look at the list of investment risks defined here and identify those you personally feel are the most important. What's an important risk? Perhaps you are most concerned about the effects of inflation or about accumulating enough money for retirement. If you are worried about inflation, you'll need to select investments that have a track record of beating inflation. If you worry about accumulating assets, you'll need to focus on setting aside as much as you can, and you'll want to invest for growth. You'll need to know which risks matter the most to you in order to make investment decisions that you are comfortable with. Taking the time to define your approach to investment risk taking will allow you to feel comfortable with the natural ups and downs of the investment markets and stay the course you've designed for yourself. If there are other risks that are important to you that are not listed here, just add them to the list on a separate piece of paper.

Managing Risk

Given the number and variety of the risks out there, it seems clear that avoiding investment risk altogether is next to impossible. What is very possible, however, is to come up with an investing plan that manages the risks you feel most strongly about and that are most relevant to your personal situation. Managing risks well is one of the important steps to becoming comfortable with your investment decision making.

Let's start with an example. Let's say you want to ride a motorcycle for the first time in your life. There are lots of things you can do to help minimize the risks associated with this event. You could take lessons from an expert, you could wear protective clothing, you could practice using the bike's control panel in your driveway, and you could watch a video about motorcycle safety. These steps really involve three things: gathering information, practicing with the new information, and taking reasonable precautions.

These are the same steps we recommend for people learning about making investing decisions. First, gather information about investments and investing—you've taken a great first step by purchasing and reading this book.

Risk Worksheet

Type of Investment Risk	Brief Definition of the Risk	Is This Risk Important to You?
Accumulation	Not accumulating enough money in time to achieve a goal.	
Business	Business cycle is bad and decreases the value of an investment.	
Credit	The person borrowing your money won't return it to you.	
Market	The market for the type of investment you own will not do well.	
Inflation	Things will continue to get more expensive.	
Interest rate	The value of an investment will change as interest rates change.	
Opportunity	A better opportunity will come along after you have committed your resources elsewhere.	
Trust and control	You put your faith in untrustworthy people.	

The more you know about the available investment choices, the more educated, comfortable decisions you'll be able to make. Knowledge will eliminate "leap of faith" thinking and replace it with comfortable decision making. You'll feel less like you're taking risks and more like you're making choices. Then practice with the information you are learning. Do the exercises in this book. Invest small amounts of money and closely follow the investments you've selected. Talk to friends about the investments they've selected.

Taking reasonable precautions, the final step in the process, is actually the easiest part of the process. You can do some, or all of the following:

- Seek expert advice. Find someone to help you make investment decisions. We'll talk about how to select an expert to help you in Part 4, Picking Investments and Professional Services.
- Choose several different types of investments. That way, if one is not doing well, others probably will be. This is the concept of diversification, which we'll talk about further.
- Keep close tabs on how your investments are doing and how their performances relate to your investment goals. We'll give you the information and tools you need to do that in Part 3, Building Your Portfolio.

A quick note: Although we did not identify them here, there are important legal and tax implications to all your investment decisions. The more money you invest, the more significant they become. The best way to find out about how these issues impact your situation is to consult an accountant or an attorney, or both.

The decision to invest, just like the decision to ride a motorcycle, is also a decision to accept a certain degree of risk. You certainly can't eliminate it, and we know it's unwise to ignore it. Your best bet is to figure out how to manage it.

6

Managing Investment Risk

Clearly, finding ways to manage investment risk is an important part of the investing process, and getting comfortable with your various risk-management options is the logical next step in the investment decision-making process.

Managing Risk through Diversification

Experts agree that the most important factor in reducing overall levels of investment risk is diversification. A dictionary definition of diversification would be to vary, to spread among different things. Diversifying investments simply means picking a few different things to invest in, rather than concentrating on just one or two areas. The simple reason for this approach is that different types of investments respond differently to the same events. So if you pick a number of investments and some do well while others don't, your returns will be an average of all of your investments, rather than just the results of just one or two things. Figure 6.1 shows how this works with equal amounts of money in two investments. As you can see, with this approach you don't receive all of the gain from Investment A in the chart, but you also don't lose nearly what you would have if all of your money was in Investment B. (Picking investments that do a little better than our Investment B wouldn't hurt either!)

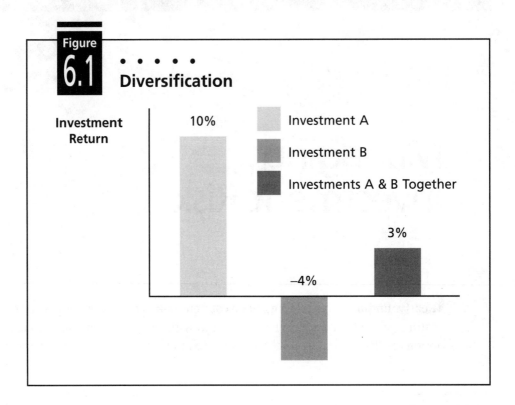

Figure 6.1 Diversification

Investment Return

10% — Investment A
Investment B
Investments A & B Together

3%

−4%

As you look at this chart, you can see that if you invested more money in Investment A, perhaps 75 percent of your account balance, and invested only 25 percent of your account balance in Investment B, you would have done much better. In fact, your return would have been 6.5 percent, rather than just 3 percent. The 3.5 percent difference in the amount of return shows how important the process of selecting different amounts of each type of investment is as well.

Developing Your Risk Management Plan— Putting It All Together

In order to make good investment selection decisions, you need to make a connection between two critical components of your personal investment risk profile and to connect them to your investment goals and your own investment strategy and plan. The two components of your personal risk profile as it relates to investing are:

1. Your comfort with risk taking—how you feel about risk—unrelated to investing
2. Investment risks—the approach you are comfortable with for balancing risk and return

Even though we are all different individuals with our own unique approach to many things, we can make some generalizations about how these two factors work together for people at different stages of their lives. This is often a great help in developing our own individual plan for managing risk.

To be sure, we know that some people get rich in unexpected ways, sometimes having both ignored the "best" advice and taken what many of us see as huge risks. Some people benefit from owning a company's stock at the "right time," or winning the lottery, or inheriting wealth. We wish these people all the best. But we can't count on the same kind of events happening to us, so we need to keep reaching for more reliable ways to build wealth, and for ways to help our money work harder.

Three Stages of Life and Risks

In the context of investing, and interacting with money, there are really three primary life stages. There are, of course, many subtle differences among people in these three stages that there are many subsets for each stage. For our purposes, we'll focus on the three primary ones. In each stage, our relationship with money and investments is different, and as a result, so is our relationship to risk, both personal and investment.

Stage One: Asset Gathering

As adults starting our careers, we are generally just beginning to interact with money in a meaningful way. This is the stage in life where people begin to earn money and have opportunities to save and invest. For many young people today the first contact with saving and investing takes place with employer-sponsored retirement plans like 401(k)s. At the same time, young people are recognizing their own financial goals. It can be a time when young people need to take on debt in order to achieve their long-term goals, like home ownership. Young people also are challenged by the twin demons of consumption and debt; balancing the ability to buy "good stuff" and the ability to use credit to buy other stuff. This cycle, as too many of us are well aware, can get you into serious financial trouble. Another hurdle to wealthbuilding at this stage is that, having just started working, it's hard to see the need to begin seriously planning for very long-term goals, like retirement.

But here's a sobering fact: The earlier you start planning to reach a long-term goal, the less money you actually need to set aside yourself. How can this be so? Compounding—the ability your money has to generate interest and earnings, and then for those earnings to grow themselves. The greatest investment risk people in this phase are dealing with is the risk of not setting realistic goals—of not taking the need for investing seriously enough and making the commitment to saving regularly. Significant, too, is the threat to their savings posed by inflation. To counter these threats, people in this phase need to begin planning for long-term goals and investing for as much return as they feel comfortable with. Here are two examples of what we mean. The first shows the difference starting the savings process early can make. As you can see, if you wait, you can never catch up, unless of course you contribute more money on a regular basis, or if your investments earn more than Mike's did in our example.

The second pitfall for investors in this phase to avoid is the trap of investing only in the very safest investments—safest that is, from the perspective of investment risk alone. The problem with this thinking is that while the least volatile investments are certainly more predictable, this predictability also means that they are most at risk from inflation. If, in Figure 6.2, Mike were to invest his assets at age 35—$12,000—in investments that earned less than 8 percent, the rate used in our example, he'd have significantly less than $184,000.

Stage Two: Asset Accumulation

After kicking off a career and settling down, most people are in, or heading toward, their peak earning years, and generally have the opportunity to set aside money earmarked for long-term saving and investing. At the same time,

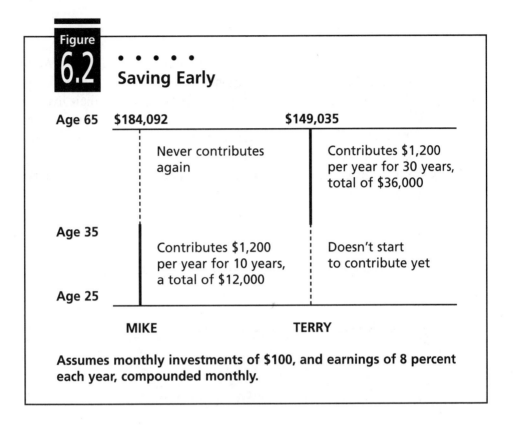

Figure 6.2 • • • • • Saving Early

Age 65	**$184,092**	**$149,035**
	Never contributes again	Contributes $1,200 per year for 30 years, total of $36,000
Age 35		
	Contributes $1,200 per year for 10 years, a total of $12,000	Doesn't start to contribute yet
Age 25		
	MIKE	**TERRY**

Assumes monthly investments of $100, and earnings of 8 percent each year, compounded monthly.

current expenses are also at their highest point, stretching household budgets. The most significant investing risks during this period are not setting aside enough money to fund long-term goals, and not investing for adequate growth. Another problem is the number of large expenses that take place at the same time for many people. For increasing numbers of older parents, college tuition bills and making significant contributions to retirement savings are concurrent expenses, causing a cash crunch, not to mention a collision of priorities. In order to avoid these traps, stage two should be a time of goal refinement and re-examination of goals to be sure that strategies are in place to meet them. Also, close attention (review every six months, at least) must be paid to investments you've selected to be sure they are delivering the returns you need with the risk you expect and are comfortable with.

Stage Three: Income Generation

Once you've reached retirement, you're in the home stretch. At this point, you are probably relying on your money to make money, rather than being dependent on earned income. Many people at this point in their lives have very little, or no, debt, and their expenses have decreased somewhat. The risks posed by this stage of life involve anything that threatens the preservation of capital and its income-generating power. Strangely enough, another huge risk is the good news that we're all living longer. This means your money has to keep up with you for a long period of time, perhaps twenty or thirty years. In order to do that, your money needs to be invested where it will keep it well ahead of inflation, or you'll run the risk of living longer than your investment account balance. Not a pleasant thought. To mitigate this risk, continue to invest your money with an eye toward the long term.

Your Relationship with Money

The purpose of this exercise is to help you to determine your current life stage and stage of relating to money, as well as the risks that accompany them. First, take a look at the Life Stages chart in Figure 6.3 that outlines each phase and its accompanying risks and strategies. Then fill in the information on Your Life Stages Worksheet on page 74, describing where you are now, your age, what is happening in your life related to money, and the risk and strategies for minimizing them that make the most sense for you. Remember that this exercise is a way to think about your "big picture" relationship with money, rather than a way to assess each financial goal and the risks and strategies for meeting them.

Figure 6.3 — Life Stages, Risks, and Investment Strategies				
Life Stage	**Approx-imate Age**	**Relationship with Money**	**Primary Investment Risks**	**Strategies for Minimizing Risks**
One: Asset gathering	20–34	• Entry-level income • Low expenses • Take on debt	• Insufficient accumulation • Inflation	• Diversification of existing assets • Goal setting
Two: Asset accumu-lation	35–64	• Increased (and perhaps steadily increasing) income • High expenses	• Insufficient accumulation • Growth • Diversification • Draining savings to fund expenses or no savings at all	• Goal refinement • Diversification
Three: Income generation (retirement)	65+	• Decreased earned income • Decreased expenses • Little or no debt	• Market risk • Diversification • Exhaust savings	• Diversification • Conservative asset growth strategy

This exercise is a tool to help you figure out your overall relationship with risk, not a way to select investments. At this point in the process, you just need to know where, in general, you are in your financial life. Because we are all different, please use the stages as a guide. You may find that you resemble a stage that doesn't correspond to your age. Don't worry about that. The whole idea of this exercise is to dig deep and get at some things that you may not even know about yourself. Things that will help you make better informed, more profitable and more comfortable investment decisions.

Your Life Stages Worksheet

Life Stage	Your Age Now	Relationship with Money	Primary Investment Risks	Strategies for Minimizing Risks

And Now, a Little More about Risk . . .

Now that you know where you are, in terms of your relationship to money, the next step is to understand the investment risks and benefits each different type of investment offers to you (see Figure 6.4). Armed with this information, you'll be able to develop a personal risk management plan, a critical piece of your investment strategy. You didn't think we were done talking about risks yet, did you?!

Figure 6.4 • • • • • **Risks and Benefits by Investment Type**	
Category and Type of Investment	***Risks, Pitfalls, and Benefits***
Cash, includes: • Savings accounts • Money market funds and deposit accounts • CDs • Your mattress	The primary risk to this category of investment is inflation. Historically, investments like these have earned only a little bit more than inflation, which does not give you the ability to grow your investments to meet long-term goals. In fact, for some people, after taxes are figured in these investments can actually lose money. However, cash investments, hands-down, offer more security than any other category of investment.
Bonds and bond funds	Bonds pay interest to bondholders. Because this is so, bond prices are greatly affected by changes in interest rates. Here's how it works. When you buy a bond, you are buying the right to receive a stated amount of income. The value of this stream of income, measured by the price of the bond, will change as investors are able to buy bonds that pay more or less income. If interest rates rise higher than the rate of interest your bond pays, the price of your bond will fall. If interest rates drop, and your bond pays a high rate of interest, its price will rise. Despite this risk, bonds do offer the most reliable stream of income, at less risk, historically speaking, than stocks. And today, there are many different kinds of bond mutual funds that offer different ways to manage the risks of interest rate changes. Another risk related to bond investing is credit risk. Because bonds are essentially loans, there is a risk that the borrower won't repay the loan. Investing in bonds and bond funds that select securities with high credit ratings is the best way to mitigate this risk. *(continued)*

Category and Type of Investment	Risks, Pitfalls, and Benefits
Individual stocks and stock funds	There are many variables that affect stocks. First, of course, is the behavior of the market overall—the market's trends affect both individual securities and funds that invest in them. Business cycles and specific events affect the securities issued by individual companies. For stock funds, both the "style" the investment managers use (their approaches to picking investments), and the type of securities they select impact the relative "riskiness" of the fund. Market capitalization is the value of all of a company's outstanding stock. Generally, companies with larger market "cap" are big, stable firms. Small "cap" stocks are shares in smaller companies. Naturally, there is more risk associated with an investment in a small, growing company than with an investment in a large, established firm. At the same time, of course, there is more opportunity for growth associated with newer, fast moving companies. There are two primary "styles" used by stock fund managers: value and growth. Value managers look for stocks that are "cheap," companies that have faced a tough market for their products and are at the beginning of a recovery cycle. Growth managers generally look for the "high flyers"—companies that will obliterate the competition. In a "down" market, value stocks have tended to drop less sharply than growth stock funds primarily because value stocks are already "cheaper" than their growth counterparts. The benefit of investing in stocks, of course, is the greatest opportunity for growth over time.

Category and Type of Investment	Risks, Pitfalls, and Benefits
Real estate • Your house • Real estate investments	Most of us who own homes are real estate investors, although we don't tend to think of ourselves that way. The risk of owning real estate is clear, that for one reason or another, it will lose its value. When we specifically buy real estate as an investment, whether we are buying a fund that invests in real estate or a rental property, the same thing is true. The benefit to buying real estate is that most people feel very confident about it—you have some idea about how to evaluate a house or building. Two rules about buying real estate this author's favorite grandpa, a real estate developer, drilled into her at a tender age: (1) Location, location, location, and (2) buy at really low prices and sell at much higher ones.

Who Me? A Real Estate Mogul?

Yes, you. People buying houses make many of the same assessments that professional investment managers make when they think about selecting investments. When you buy a house you:

- Assess interest rates when you decide to take out a variable or fixed-rate mortgage
- Evaluate market conditions
- Pick a price you are willing to pay for the house

Investment managers evaluate:

- Interest rates
- Market conditions
- Prices for individual securities

Time

The time frames for your investment goals impact how much investment risk you are willing or able to take to achieve a given goal. Look at Figure 6.5 to see the traditional investment risk and return relationship. This figure shows that the further away the goal, the more sense it makes to take on increased investment risk—and the increased opportunity for investment return that goes along with it.

The further away the goal, the less impact traditional investment risks of volatility and fluctuation of value will have. And, at the same time, the greater is the benefit of increased investment return. For goals that are rapidly approaching, it makes much more sense to take on the risk of inflation, and to put the savings in the most stable investment available.

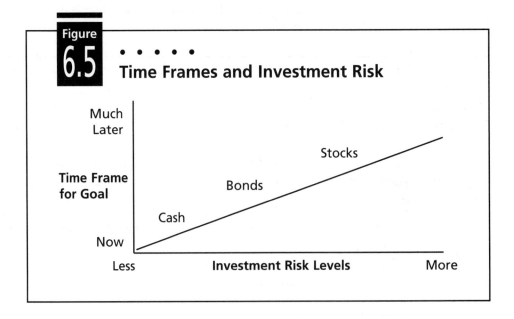

Figure 6.5 • • • • • **Time Frames and Investment Risk**

7

Connecting Risk to Your Decisions about Investing

At this point, we've talked a lot about risks, both personal risk and different kinds of investment risks that impact your decision making. In order to put some of these ideas about risk into practice, it is helpful to see the connection to different kinds of investments and investment mixes.

There are also (of course!) different labels that the investment industry applies to people in different life stages. These labels are used to help investment professionals develop an appropriate investment strategy for their clients, and are used a lot in the financial press. We think it's helpful to give you the information behind the labels, so you can understand what drives these recommendations.

Let's talk for a minute about the three core risk categories you'll hear the most about:

1. The aggressive investor
2. The moderate, or middle-of-the-road, investor
3. The conservative investor

The Aggressive Investor

These folks are typically characterized as younger and having ambitious long-term goals, corresponding to Stage One, Asset Gathering. They might choose investments offering both high levels of risk and the opportunity for big returns.

The Moderate, or Middle-of-the-Road, Investor

This type of investor, corresponding to Stage Two, Asset Accumulation, generally wants the safety of having some money in predictable investments where the principal is sure to be there when they need it, but is equally focused in growing their money over the long haul. Investment recommendations might focus on both fixed-income investments and more conservative stock funds.

The Conservative Investor

Generally, the connection is made here to investors in Stage Three, Income Generation. The core assumption is that there is a very short time to save (or no time at all) and that major swings in the principal amount of their investments are very undesirable. Better to know the money is there, hopefully keeping ahead of inflation, than to try to achieve big gains.

Recap of Investment Choices

Figure 7.1 recaps the life stages, risk categories, and the corresponding investment mixes. As you review this chart, keep in mind what we've said before—your personal risk tolerance may not necessarily correspond with what the "experts" say it should be at your particular life phase. There are many young people who prefer a less risky approach, but may have to be more aggressive with their long-term goals. There are also many older people who prefer to "play the market" and don't want to use a conservative approach but still have to manage an income stream in retirement. Again, this chart shows the typical mix for the different phases of life as recommended by investment experts.

Risk Is about Feelings, Too

We've made the point before, but we'd like to show you what we mean. Deciding how you feel about investment risk is a very personal process, illustrated by two stories an investment professional friend of ours likes to tell.

Figure 7.1	• • • • • **Life Stage, Risk Category, and Investment Mix Chart**

Life Stage	Risk Category	Typical Investment Mix
Asset gathering	Aggressive	Mostly stocks and stock funds, some fixed-income and little cash.
Asset accumulation	Moderate	Split between fixed-income and conservative stock funds.
Income generation	Conservative	Primarily fixed-income and cash, some stocks for growth.

One of her clients is a very wealthy 96-year-old woman named Elaine. Our adviser friend has spent lots of time with her client discussing the various risks associated with different kinds of investments. At this point, you might see Elaine in the income generation stage, as a conservative investor. But not Elaine. Based on her personal feelings about risk and investing, they have put all of her money into the stock market. She lost more than $500,000 in October of 1987. By her 96th birthday, she had recovered that and her portfolio was up by another $6.5 million dollars.

Another client is 37, single with no kids. She has a high-level job and has saved great sums of money. She is extremely uncomfortable with the idea of investment risk. Her investments? All fixed income and cash.

While these investment choices defy the conventional approach recommended by the experts and the asset allocation models out there, they make excellent sense to the investors. The moral of the stories? Make investment decisions that make sense *and* that make you feel comfortable. Remember the whole idea behind money? It's something to trade for other things that you need and want. We don't know any people who want to actually pay for added stress and anxiety!

A Nontraditional View

We've outlined here both the three life stages of investing and the three traditional risk categories for investors. These are the most common ways to consider what types of investments make sense to select. We'd like to suggest another way to approach this discussion, involving your goals and values. Look back to Chapter 1 where you set your financial goals and noted the values you associate with those goals. Wouldn't it make more sense to link your investment choices and their risk implications to the individual goals you've set for yourself? This approach would allow a young investor to separate out her important goal of saving the money to buy a home in five years and invest accordingly. She would be able to see the distinction between this conservative goal and her other goals, retirement for example, that would suggest a more aggressive investment approach.

The approach to risk that most supports how our lives actually work involves looking at goals and values, and, taking into consideration personal feelings about risk, designing an investment portfolio that will best help you meet these goals. This approach allows you to consider your own general personal risk management approach *and* still look at each of your goals and the risk you need to assume to meet them independently.

Taking Educated Risk to Meet Goals

Using the list you developed of your goals, dollar amounts, and time frames to meet them in Part 1, put each of the goals in the top box of the Allocating Money Based on Goals, Time, and Risk Worksheet below, in priority order, beginning with your most important goal. In the box next to the goal, fill in the time frame until you expect to reach this goal. Next to the goal and the time frame, write down a couple of investments that make sense to you, that will help you meet this goal, given the information you've learned so far. In Part 3 of the book, Building Your Portfolio, we'll fine tune these selections based on investment performance information, so don't worry about being too precise. The goal is simply to gain a perspective about which investments make sense relative to your individual goals.

Looking at each of the goals and investment approaches, do you see some consistency or does your strategy vary considerably? Sometimes with larger goals, you will have several individual accounts designated for those goals. An individual account that has a specific goal attached makes the appropriate investment allocation decision for that account much easier. For smaller goals, you may have mingled your money into a single account. Take a look at your list: Is there a consistent theme in the way you have invested your money?

Now, perhaps most importantly, thinking about your own personal approach to risk taking, do the allocations you've selected match your own approach to risk? You may have considered yourself to be a risk taker and yet find yourself gravitating toward the least risky investments. Or perhaps the opposite is true. Well fine, you might say, what do I do now? Unless that approach means you'll have a hard time meeting your goals (we'll talk more about this in Part 3), and/or your current strategy is causing you stress there's no need to do anything. You have, we suggest, just learned an interesting fact about yourself, something very important. This is where the two pieces of the puzzle—personal risk taking and investment risk—come together, where the rubber meets the road, so to speak. This is where you need to take the information you've learned about the facts of investment risk, and temper it with your own feelings and perceptions.

• • • • •

Allocating Money Based on Goals, Time, and Risk Worksheet

Goal (in priority order)	Time Frame	Investment Mix
1. *College education for oldest child*	*Fourteen years*	*75% in growth stock mutual fund, 25% in bond mutual fund*
2.		
3.		
4.		
5.		
6.		
7.		

In the example above, the first priority is to save for a child's college education. Although the child is now only four years old and fourteen years seems a long time to save, in reality the investment approach needs to be fairly conservative. The money must be there at a certain time, there is little flexibility. The investment approach, therefore, should include the opportunity to make a reasonable return through stock mutual funds that focus on growth stocks and should also include a conservative investment like bonds. The cost of college education has risen much faster than the rate of inflation so a pure savings account, or other conservative investment mix, could leave this child without the money he or she needs at college time.

The risks that need to be considered in this example include the risk of inflation (rising cost of college), the risk related to having a specific time when the money is needed (no opportunity to delay the date), and the risk of not saving enough for the child to have a choice of what college to attend. Each goal that you set will have its own list of risks attached. The challenge is to balance the inherent risks in the goal with your own personal risk tolerance and then, when choosing the investments for the goal, understand the risks that go along with each of the investments you've selected. As we've said before, risk is unavoidable in the investment process. The only thing that makes it easier to deal with is understanding more about it.

Now that you understand more about risk, you can make more "risk informed" investment decisions. Of course, ultimately you won't see or touch the investments you select, you will only be able to read the materials, or talk to someone about them. This may mean that you never really feel comfortable with the risks involved. The process is really no different from selecting a new model car the first year it is manufactured. You read the materials that evaluate the car, decide if its features are right for you, and finally make the decision to buy the car, probably based in part on your own feeling of confidence about the product and the manufacturer. Buying investments works the same way.

Investments You Have Picked to Date

This exercise gives you the opportunity to look at the investment selections you have made to date and why you have made them. The idea here is to give you a framework for understanding the investment risks you are choosing to take with your existing portfolio of investments, and to find out if that's really where you want to be. Because you'll lay out your investments in a picture, this exercise will help you "see" your approach to investment risk.

To start, list on a separate piece of paper all of the different investments you have selected to date. Remember to include any investment choices you have made in a 401(k) plan, IRA, or other type of account. If you can recall, include the dates that you made the investments and if you have done so, when they were sold.

Now take a look at your list and consider why you made the choices that you did. Next to each investment, write down the financial goals you were trying to accomplish by choosing each investment. Note also if you were guided in making any of these decisions by a financial expert, friend, or coworker. Also, note any risks that you were aware you were taking, or trying to avoid, by making each of these choices.

Now, take a look at the original list. Knowing more now than you probably did when you made these choices, would you make the same ones over again?

Another step in the process of evaluating your investments is to map them across the risk/return continuum chart. This is another way for you to be certain that you have selected investments that will help you reach your goals. Figure 7.2 shows a Risk/Return Continuum chart that is filled in with the three main categories of investments. Figure 7.3 is a blank chart you can use to fill in your own investments. This is a quick and simple way to literally "see" where most of your investments fall on the spectrum. You might want to make several copies of this page so you can use the chart as often as you like.

To complete the chart, turn back to the list of investments you just made. Now, take each investment and write it in on the blank Risk/Return Continuum chart. Remember the information we've covered about investment risk and re-

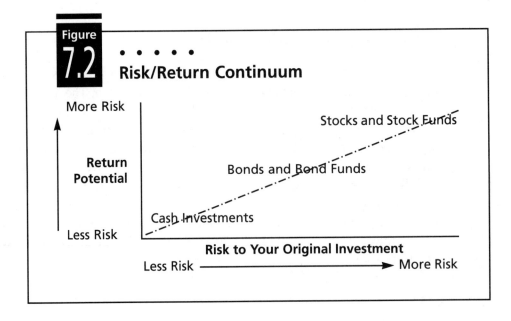

Figure 7.2 • • • • •
Risk/Return Continuum

More Risk

Return Potential

Less Risk

Stocks and Stock Funds

Bonds and Bond Funds

Cash Investments

Risk to Your Original Investment
Less Risk ⟶ More Risk

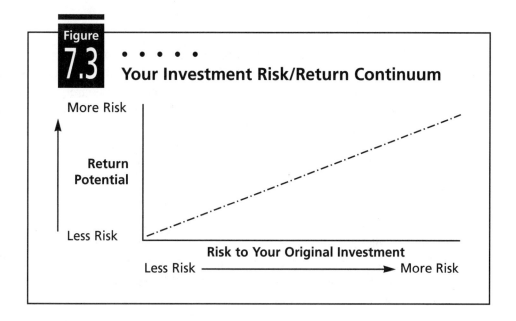

Figure 7.3

• • • • •

Your Investment Risk/Return Continuum

More Risk

Return Potential

Less Risk

Risk to Your Original Investment

Less Risk ─────────────────────▶ More Risk

fer back to other material if you need to. This is not meant to be a mathematical analysis; rather, it is simply a way to help you see the decisions you've made within the framework of investment risk, so don't worry if you're not sure precisely where each investment falls. Fill in the chart as best you can.

Here are a few more tips about how to categorize your investments. Generally, individual securities are considered to have greater risk than mutual funds, because mutual funds hold lots of securities and are themselves diversified portfolios. Investments in each asset class also can be sorted according to degree of risk and potential for return. Not all bond funds are the same, nor are all money markets equal. If it's helpful, try to rank all of the investments you hold in each asset class in risk/return order before filling in the chart. Here's some more information about organizing your investments.

Stocks and Stock Mutual Funds

The stocks of larger companies are generally considered to be less risky than the stocks of smaller companies. Likewise, stocks of older, more established companies are generally thought to be less of a risk than stocks of newer, more adventurous companies.

Bonds and Bond Mutual Funds

Like loans, the longer the term (length of the repayment period) of a bond, the greater the risk it generally carries, and the more return (or interest) it will likely offer. On the other hand, shorter term bonds are generally perceived to carry less risk. Another risk factor for bonds is the ability of the borrower to repay its debts. If a bond issuer is seen as less able to repay the bond, the bond will be seen as having higher risk and will pay a higher rate of return.

Cash Investments

Although this category of investment is generally seen as carrying the least risk, distinctions among cash investments can be made. Remember that this category includes cash and securities that can be converted to cash quickly. Here again, the length of time the security will be held and the borrower's ability to repay are considerations.

PART 3

Building Your Portfolio

Let's take just a minute to review how we've gotten to where we are now. So far, we've talked about the importance of, and process for, establishing financial and investment goals. We've also talked about the important concepts of investment risk and personal risk as they relate to developing your investment plan.

At this point, there are two more steps in the investment decision-making process. The first is how to create and develop an investment portfolio. To do this, you'll need an understanding of how available investments work together to meet long-term financial goals. This will help you to make investment selections and decisions based on the four criteria for making investment decisions: your goals; investment risks; the cost of your goals; and what the different types of investments offer to you. That's the focus of Part Three of this book.

The final steps in the investment decision-making process are to establish appropriate investment accounts for yourself, find additional information or hire additional help and support, and pick investments that will support your personal financial goals. We'll cover that in Part Four, Picking Investments and Professional Services.

Let's begin by looking first at the different types of investments that are available.

8

Asset Classes

In many other industries, products are labeled by their function. In the appliance business, a washing machine washes things, a dryer dries. In the investment industry, most things are labeled using what we call industry-speak, or jargon. Your best bet? Learn the language! In order to make good investment decisions, you first have to understand the terminology the pros use, then you can easily learn about the products.

The phrase "asset class" is used to describe categories of investments. This is another way to say "types of investments." There are many different asset classes. You can invest in stocks and bonds, gold, antique cars, stamps, or baseball cards, to name just a few. In the investment industry, there are three core categories of investments—asset classes—that most people choose to invest in:

1. Equities (i.e., stocks)
2. Fixed income (i.e., bonds)
3. Cash investments (i.e., bank savings account)

Because you can create a well-rounded portfolio with the three core asset classes, and because narrowing the field a bit will help you develop a comfort level with making investment decisions, we'll focus our discussion here on building a portfolio with stocks, bonds, and cash investments.

Cash and Money Market Investments

Cash and other investments that are very "liquid," meaning that they can be sold for cash almost immediately, fall into this category. Because there is typically so little risk that the value of cash investments will change, they generally earn the lowest interest or returns of any kind of investment. Bank CDs, savings accounts, money market funds and deposit accounts, and savings bonds are all examples of cash investments. Money market mutual funds generally maintain a stable ($1.00) net asset value (we'll talk more about net asset values in Chapter 18), meaning that the value of your initial investment is not likely to change. Because you know exactly what return to expect, and because there's almost no risk of losing your invested money, cash and cash-type investments can be a useful place to put money you are planning to use very soon, say within six months or a year.

Bonds and Bond Funds

Bonds are a loan of money to a company or government entity. In return for borrowing your money, bond issuers pay regular interest income and must repay the bondholder (you) the amount they borrowed, called the "face amount" of the bond. Because bonds pay interest, the price of a bond (the amount you could sell it for) changes when the interest rate set by the Federal Reserve Bank (the "Fed") changes, or when the borrower's ability to repay the bond changes.

Bond prices and interest rates have an interesting and confusing relationship. To simplify this, picture a see-saw. When one end goes up, the other goes down. Both ends cannot be up at the same time. Bond prices work the same way. If the Fed increases rates so that the rate of interest on other bonds being sold rises above the rate you are being paid, the price of your bond will fall. If the rate you are being paid is higher than the new rate set by the Fed, your bond will be worth more. Depending on where interest rates are, bonds are generally less risky than stocks. And keep in mind, that even though the "value" of your bond goes up and down with interest rates, you still receive the rate that you expected to when you purchased the bond. You also will receive the "face value" (amount that is listed on the face of the bond) at its maturity. With a bond, the face value and the interest rate is fixed and predictable; what changes is the "value" of the bond. When interest rates change, your bond is worth more or less because a higher rate on your bond is more attractive when rates go lower and a lower rate on your bond is less attractive when rates go higher. Because of the fact that bonds typically generate a stream of predictable income over time, many retirement investors choose them.

Some bonds offer tax advantages as well, and they are useful for investors needing a tax break. Bonds offered by states and municipalities (cities and towns) are exempt from federal tax, while U.S. Treasury bonds are exempt from state income taxes. The tax benefits effectively increase the yield from these types of bonds, and especially if you're in a high tax bracket, they are well worth examining closely.

You can buy individual bonds yourself or you can invest in a bond fund. Bonds tend to be fairly expensive to buy individually, generally costing $1,000 each, and sometimes as much as $10,000. The advantage to buying bonds individually is that you will receive regular interest payments from the bond issuer for the life of the bond *and* if you hold the bond until maturity, you'll get back what you paid for it, too. Bonds have different maturities, anywhere from 1 to 40 years. In general, the longer the term of the bond, the more volatile its price. If you want to generate income over a long period of time and minimize your risk, you might consider "laddering" maturities. This means buying bonds for your portfolio that mature at different times, for example, six months, one year, and two years. Laddering is one way to diversify a bond portfolio. A cautionary note, in general: Longer maturities do not pay a significant enough amount of additional interest to warrant the risk of holding them longer.

As an alternative, bond funds invest in many bonds, pooling investors' money. Each bond fund has a specific objective and invests money according to a stated investment strategy. Bond funds are sensitive to interest rates and other factors, as we discussed earlier. As a result, the principal you invest in a bond fund could be at risk, perhaps more so than with an investment in an individual bond. Bond funds, like other type of pooled investments, do offer the important benefit of diversification.

Stocks and Stock Funds

Also called shares, stocks represent ownership in a company. Investments in stocks can grow two different ways. First, many stocks pay dividends (distributions of corporate earnings) to the people who own them (stockholders). Second, as companies grow and their businesses become bigger and more profitable, the price of a stock may go up, and you can sell your stock at a profit.

Like bonds, you can buy stocks individually or you can buy a stock fund. Choosing individual stocks can be fun for many investors, and if you know enough about the company you are choosing to invest in, can be very rewarding. It does, however, take a time commitment to invest in individual stocks because it is necessary to understand a company and the industry it's in before you invest. Because of the built-in diversification that stock mutual funds offer, as well as the professional expertise of fund managers, stock mutual funds have become overwhelmingly popular.

To meet different investment needs, investment managers can tailor stock funds a number of different ways to mirror or manipulate the market's risk and return characteristics. Because stock funds are clearly the most volatile asset class available to investors, stock funds generally vary from stable to very aggressive. As a rule of thumb, a very aggressive fund will often mean greater specialization in the fund, for example, a specific segment of industry, like technology, or an emerging market like Eastern Europe. This can mean that the fund manager has a narrower focus of specific companies and stocks to choose from. It could also mean that the manager is focusing on several different industries, but only companies of a certain risk profile. These types of funds will have a higher risk level associated with them. And of course, the higher the risk level, the greater the return potential. Stock funds that invest in large companies tend to be the least volatile stock funds, and therefore considered the least risky. Index funds (discussed below), which have become increasingly popular, generally mirror the market. A portfolio manager of a fund which is not an index fund will try to "beat" the overall market by using a specific strategy of where and when to invest, while an index manager just tries to match what the market is doing on average. Small company stock funds, international funds, and sector funds that focus on a particular industry or part of the economy are, again, the more aggressive types of stock funds.

Indexes

The Dow Jones Industrials and the Standard & Poor's 500 often make headlines. Nonetheless, most people don't know what they are or why what they do is so important. So what are they? What do they mean? Both are indexes of stock market performance. Their job, so to speak, is to take the temperature of different segments of the stock market, to see whether prices are going up or down or standing still. These indexes, and many others, simply track how the market itself, or a segment of the market, performs. An index will tell you how the market is doing, and importantly, how it has done over an extended period of time. There are indexes for different types of stocks, for bonds, for cash, for international investments, etc. When you look at different investments, especially mutual funds, be sure to look at the index the fund manager is trying to "beat." Indexes are often called benchmarks.

Why are benchmarks important? They are a way for investors—and investment managers—to evaluate how they are doing. Because benchmarks represent unmanaged (i.e., no one is doing anything to influence the outcome) investment performance, and investment managers are paid to manage money, logically, they should be able to beat their benchmark. Over time, outstanding investment managers will be able to beat their benchmarks consistently. Few managers are able to beat their benchmarks every year, however, with most doing so in some years and not in others. In a down year, where the market benchmarks are down in the negative numbers, look to good investment managers to lose less than the market overall.

You can't invest directly in an index itself, but you can select mutual funds that try to mirror the index, like S&P 500 funds, and funds that try to mirror all or part of the Dow Jones fund index. The Dow Jones Industrial Average is made up of 30 of the largest industrial companies in America. The important point is that for whatever investments you choose, you'll need to know what the comparable benchmarks for performance are, and to keep an eye on how your funds are doing in relative terms.

International Investments

All of the different types of investments you have just read about—cash, stocks and bonds and all of their subcategories—can be issued by companies based in or outside the United States. Securities issued by companies beyond our borders are generally described as international investments. There are many excellent reasons to look at international investment opportunities.

Today, companies located beyond our borders make many of the things we buy and use. In order to participate in the growth that our purchases generate for these companies, we must invest abroad as well. Investing money in companies overseas means you can take advantage of all of the changes happening worldwide. You will also know that, should the economy at home slow down for any reason, your investments will still have an opportunity to grow globally. International investing is one of the best ways to diversify the investments in your portfolio.

There are, of course, different risks associated with international investing. Economies in countries that are just developing, or that have developed to a degree and are becoming part of the global economy, tend to be fragile. Their currencies can be susceptible to fluctuation, changing the costs of things they import and export. Political environments can change, suddenly making it harder—or easier—to do business in a certain place. Because we are living in such a global environment, it's hard not to recognize the international influence everywhere around us, and investing is part of this influence. There is no doubt that international investing is important to all investors. Keep in mind too, that if you're Italian, Italy is not "international," nor is Russia "international" to Russians. Every economy is home to the people who invest there.

One distinction that needs to be made here is between international funds and global funds. In theory, an international fund invests all of its money outside of the United States borders while a global fund can invest in both U.S. and non-U.S. securities. We say, "in theory" because you need to read the prospectus on a fund. Many international funds have the ability to invest a certain percentage of their money in U.S. securities. You need to know how much this is so you can do a better job of diversifying and make sure you don't have too many eggs in the same investment baskets.

Real Estate

Although it's not one of the three core asset classes addressed here, we also have talked about real estate as an investment opportunity, in Chapter 6. Because for most of us investments in real estate are limited to our homes, we won't go into much more detail. Suffice it to say again, be sure to recognize that you have "invested" in your home and realize the risk and reward implications associated with having too much, or too little, money of your total portfolio invested there.

Returns

Returns are the numbers that quantify the growth (or loss) a specific investment has experienced. Annual returns tell you how an investment did over a one-year period. Compound returns reflect the total effect of a number of years' performance on a particular investment or portfolio of investments. Average returns are simply the average of a number of years' performance. Yield is the amount of income an investment earns, most often seen on bonds or other fixed-income instruments like certificates of deposit. Total return is the sum of any income an investment generates, plus the gain (or loss) from its sale.

Investing in Stocks and Bonds Over Time

Your investment goals will be the primary guide for your approach to building an investment portfolio, but central to the idea of investing well is the concept of preserving your capital over time—or shall we say, not losing what you've started with and earned! Inflation—increases in the cost of goods and services over time—is the biggest threat to your money. For the past fifty years or so, inflation has averaged around 3 percent per year. This is a good reminder that, while you may have selected some "safe" investments that are not beating inflation by a wide margin, it is important to select some that offer you the opportunity for greater returns over time.

By comparison, large company stocks have historically returned around 11 percent per year, while corporate bonds have returned in the range of 5 percent on average, according to Ibbotson Associates. Remember that returns for stocks and bonds are volatile—they can move around quite a bit. The reason to be aware of this is that, over the short run, you may need to use your money just when your stock fund—or the market as a whole—has taken a dip. This is why it makes sense not to invest too much of your overall portfolio in the market unless you are taking a longer term view. You don't want to place yourself in the position of needing your money desperately just when the investment has taken a dive. You want to be able to take money from other, less volatile, places while you wait (and hope and pray) that the fund, or the market, comes back.

The Market for Your Money

All of our discussion so far has focused on making investment decisions from the perspective of the purchaser of investments: you, the investor. There is another equally important perspective, the one that belongs to the person or company or entity using your money. To get a complete picture of how different kinds of investments behave—what they do and why—it is important to know what happens to your money when you give it to someone else to use.

How Companies Finance Themselves

Companies need money to operate. Some of this money comes from the money they earn by selling their products or services and making a profit on the sale. Often, in order to compete effectively, at a given point in time companies need more money than they are able to generate by selling their goods and services. When this happens, companies generally have two options: share the ownership of their company with others who will give them money for it, or borrow money.

Towns and other government entities experience a similar need for cash to undertake large projects. These groups have the ability to raise money by offering bonds for sale to investors. These bonds are repaid with tax revenues.

On the other side of the fence are people who want to invest their money so that it grows substantially. Now we have someone who needs money, a buyer, and someone who has money to lend, a seller. With people and companies needing money, and people and companies offering money, a market is created. Investors use their money to buy the stocks and bonds that companies, or other entities, issue. The companies use the money individuals invest to help run and grow their businesses.

Stocks

Companies that choose to issue stock are comfortable with the idea of sharing the ownership of their company with others. Companies that are private and then issue stock are described as "going public." This just means that the public now has access to the company's stock and stockholders have a say in how the company is run.

Once a company has issued stock, its stock will be traded on a stock exchange. The New York Stock Exchange and the American Stock Exchange are two you might have heard about. When people who own stock sell it to someone else, the sales price is paid to the owner of the stock, rather than the company that originally issued it.

Companies whose stocks are traded publicly generally provide a lot of information about how their company is doing to the public and to the Wall Street community. If the company is doing well, the value of its stock will reflect its success. Weaknesses will be reflected as well. Not all private companies welcome this kind of continuous scrutiny and so may look for a way other than issuing stock to raise money.

Bonds

When a company needs money but doesn't want to give up any ownership in the company to investors, it can issue bonds, or debt. When you own a company's bond, you are entitled to be paid a specific interest rate and on a specific date to be repaid the amount of money you loaned the company. The downside to the issuer of debt is that it always has to be repaid.

The company is, in effect, borrowing money from investors for the period of time it thinks it needs it. When the bond is paid off, at maturity, the company has no further obligation to bondholders. It is important to have an assurance that a company issuing bonds will be able to pay you the interest it owes and to repay the bond when it comes due. If the company is likely to pay, and therefore considered to be less of a risk, your interest rate is lower. If the company is a "credit risk," your anticipated rate of return likely will be higher. Like stocks, people who own bonds can sell them to one another in the bond market.

What Would You Do to Raise Money?

Another perspective to evaluating the relative merits of stocks and bonds is the perspective of the issuer, the "creator," so to speak, of the securities. The following exercise allows you to get comfortable, from the issuer's perspective, with why you might issue stocks versus bonds, or vice versa, to raise money for your business.

It's Your Company

This exercise will give you a better understanding of where stocks and bonds come from in the first place, and what decisions a company or government entity needs to think about when it needs money. Imagine that you are running your own company manufacturing some kind of gadget that is meaningful to you. This company was a vision you had and is now a successful, highly profitable operation. But, like many businesses with great ideas and great opportunities, you don't have the money in your current cash flow to match the opportunity out there. You must raise capital for your business by issuing either stocks or bonds. To this point, your company has been private, so you must mull over a number of things as you consider how best to get the money you need.

(continued)

In the Financing Choices Worksheet below, list the pros and cons to you as the owner of the business that you might face when you decide to issue either stock or bonds to raise the money you need. Refer back to the section preceding this exercise to get some ideas of what you might need to consider.

• • • • •

Financing Choices Worksheet

Method of Financing	Benefits to Company and Owner	Potential Downside to Company and Owner
Stocks		
Bonds		

Same Company—Different Ways to Use Money

When considering whether to buy a stock or bond, or deciding which company to invest in, it is important to understand both the differences between various types of investments and the company you are investing in.

The value of stocks is tied to a company's performance, but companies are not required to pay a dividend to the holders of their stock, even in a good year. Companies issuing bonds are obligated to pay bondholders interest and principal (your original investment), but the value of a bond is not related to how well a company is doing. As noted earlier, it's related to what is happening with interest rates.

Whether you choose stocks or bonds, you want to choose to invest in a company or industry that you feel comfortable with. Is the company performing well in its industry? Is it positioned to take advantage of industry changes? Is it in strong financial shape? Is it in a booming—or busting—industry? The most important thing you can do is ask as many questions as you need to to feel comfortable about the companies that will be using your money. Don't invest in something just because someone told you it's a "sure bet." Take the time to learn as much as you can about the company and industry.

Dollar Cost Averaging

Over time, dollar cost averaging helps the natural ups and downs of the investment markets work to your benefit. Here's how. Let's assume that monthly you invest a fixed amount of money, say $50, in a mutual fund. Your total investment is $600 for the year. Now, take a look at Figure 9.1. In this case, $600 purchased $609.53 worth of mutual fund shares.

Because share prices fluctuate, the average share price you paid may be lower than the price you would have paid if you had bought all your shares at one time.

In addition to meaning that over time you pay less, on average, for an investment, dollar cost averaging is a great way to set up periodic payments to an investment account and to accumulate money by doing so a little at a time.

Figure 9.1 • • • • •
Dollar Cost Averaging Chart

Month	Share Price	Number of Shares Purchased
January	20.00	2.5
February	22.11	2.26
March	23.00	2.17
April	20.41	2.45
May	23.86	2.10
June	27.67	1.81
July	24.49	2.04
August	28.10	1.78
September	27.85	1.81
October	26.46	1.89
November	27.10	1.85
December	28.32	1.77
	24.95 **Average Share Price** (total of $299.37 share price divided by 12 months)	**24.43** **Total Number of** **Shares Purchased**

Diversification and Asset Allocation

Now that you have a frame of reference for evaluating different kinds of investments, the word "diversification" will make a lot of sense. The concept of diversification is very simple: don't buy just one kind of investment. Why? If you choose just one thing, you'll limit your ability to take advantage of the best performing markets, and you may lock yourself into one of the poorer performers at the same time. The idea may be simple, but the reasons from an investment perspective that make diversification make so much sense are not so simple.

The three core asset categories we've talked about (stocks, bonds, and cash) have very different uses and purposes. As a result, they behave very differently. They behave, or respond, to three different categories of changes:

1. Company-level changes—stocks and bonds are issued by companies that can experience changes in how their businesses operate, for better or for worse. You could have purchased the bond or the stock when the company was operating under one set of financial conditions and, while you still own your investment, the company could change a little or a lot.
2. Market-specific changes—the markets, both stock and bond, themselves respond to overall economic shifts and predictions.
3. Broad economic changes—including interest rates, employment, and currency shifts.

Of course, while broad economic changes affect all of us, and probably all of the different categories of investments, at the same time, they may not create the same reaction in each of the different types of investments available. In fact, the same information may produce different—even opposite—reactions in different markets. It's getting harder to predict how different economic changes will affect different categories of investments. The best bet is not to try to "time" the market, or "psyche out" the predictions but rather insulate yourself by diversifying across investment types.

To make good investment decisions, you simply need to choose investments from each of the broad asset categories to invest in. You certainly don't need to watch closely and react to changes in all of the companies or markets you invest in, or even the broad economy. Simply diversifying your investments across the investment marketplace will provide you with the most important benefit: not having all of your eggs in one basket.

OK. So that's the basic concept. Now we'll focus on how to take this idea and use it to make good investment decisions. Asset allocation is simply investment-speak for using the concept of diversification to guide your decision-making process. When you allocate your assets, you simply decide how much of one or another investment you'll choose; 50 percent of this, 20 percent of that, and 30 percent of something else, for example. You can allocate your assets all together, as one portfolio, or you can allocate the assets you have invested for each individual goal you have set for yourself.

Two things you should know: first, why asset allocation and diversification work, and second, how to use them effectively to reach your goals.

Understanding Diversification and Asset Allocation

As we've said, different kinds of investments behave differently, depending on a number of factors. Some may increase in value, others decrease. If you have only one kind of investment in your portfolio, whatever happens to that one investment determines what happens to your portfolio overall. If you choose investments from different asset categories, however, the value of your total portfolio will change less dramatically if only one part of it changes in value. Spreading your investment means you have a good chance of a higher return than "too safe" investments, while avoiding the danger of losing your entire investment.

As you know, the three primary asset classes are stocks (or equities), bonds (or fixed income), and money market investments (cash equivalents). Figure 10.1 shows what happens to two different investments at the same point in time. As you can see, investment A is moving in one direction, investment B in another. The degree to which different asset classes move (or don't move) together is called correlation. In order to benefit from the positive movements and limit the impact of the negative ones, you'll need to choose some of each investment. And look what happens when you do that: the portfolio—your investments, all together—has better, more stable performance than either investment on its own. Of course, we're using a hypothetical example here rather than real investments, just to make our point. But you can easily see the benefit we're talking about.

Asset allocation, as we've said, is the process of determining what percentage of each kind of investment your portfolio should hold. The asset allocation process quantifies (calculates) the risk and return associated with each investment in a portfolio and suggests investments in certain products based on

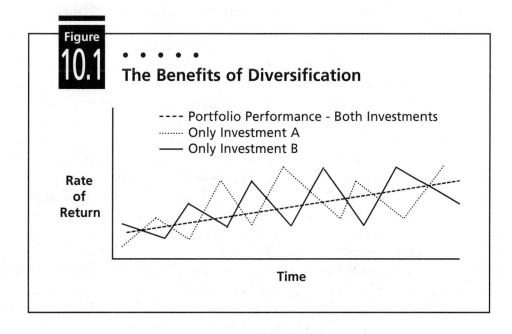

Figure 10.1

• • • • •
The Benefits of Diversification

- - - - Portfolio Performance - Both Investments
········· Only Investment A
——— Only Investment B

Rate of Return

Time

a number of different factors, including investment performance, risk factors, time frames, and goals. You can do simple asset allocation yourself; we'll show you how in Chapter 11. The pros generally use sophisticated software programs to do asset allocation based on historical investment performance. Why all the fuss about asset allocation? Investment professionals see the asset allocation decision as one of the most important investment decisions they make and estimate that it accounts for much of a portfolio's overall performance.

You can diversify the investments in your portfolio in many different ways, including:

- Across asset classes
- Choosing investments with different investment management styles
- Varying the industries from which you select investments
- Choosing investments that have different time frames
- Choosing investments with different ratings
- Picking investments from different countries
- Varying the investment firms from which you buy products

A Personal Approach to Building Your Own Portfolio

We've talked a lot about making specific decisions with which you can be comfortable. Another way to pay attention to your comfort level is to approach your life as an investor the same way you approach your personal life. In other words, if you tend to have a lot of things going on every day—and you like that—you may want to have lots of different investment accounts with lots of different investments in them. By the same token, if you have too much going on with too little focus on any one thing, you can dilute your overall effectiveness. More, by and of itself, is not necessarily better, but you may be a person who can handle more and who likes to do so. On the other hand, if you prefer a quieter existence, with less activity, you might want to limit the number of accounts and investments you work with. Just be sure you have enough different pieces to make the overall picture effective.

No approach is either "right" or "wrong." Both are perfectly valid and do not, in any way, limit your ability to set and achieve financial goals. The key here is to choose investments that make sense to you and that together, will help you set and achieve financial goals over the long haul.

Mental Barriers to Making Investment Decisions

Increasingly, the investment and financial services industry is recognizing how important our feelings and ideas about money are to the investment decision-making process. Many of us fall into the habit of mentally segmenting or classifying money by placing it into different "buckets." This is something most of us have experienced when we receive cash gifts or inheritances. We've certainly talked to a number of investors who have experienced this. Because the money is "unexpected," it's OK to just spend it, or to invest in something that we see as having a very high level of investment risk. Money we've saved up over time, however, we tend to feel a greater sense of ownership for, and consequently, invest it more conservatively. Interesting, don't you think? Is money we've earned ourselves any different than money that someone else has given us? A dollar is still a dollar at the end of the day.

When we receive a gift of cash, especially a small sum, we tend to spend it on ourselves and buy something we like. We talked with one woman who had cashed every birthday and holiday gift check she'd ever received and saved the money without spending a dime of it. Most of these gifts were in $10, $25, and $50 increments. After several years of doing this with every gift, she had close to $1,500 saved in a bureau drawer. Instead of spending it all on some big item, she chose to fund her first investment account with it. Are you receiving any "small" sums of money you can save instead of spend, and then invest?

Allocating Your Own Assets to Meet Your Investment Goals

Here's where you actually start to make some investment decisions for yourself. You'll be well on your way to making the kinds of investment decisions you'd like for yourself after you consider the following four factors:

1. The time frame for achieving your goal
2. The relative cost of your goal
3. Investment performance
4. Your comfort with risk

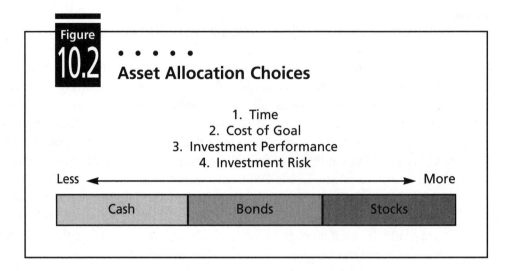

Figure 10.2

• • • • •

Asset Allocation Choices

1. Time
2. Cost of Goal
3. Investment Performance
4. Investment Risk

Less ← ——————————————————→ More

| Cash | Bonds | Stocks |

Here is a picture of how these four factors might point you in the direction of different asset allocation choices.

Let's look more closely at each of the factors in our asset allocation decision.

Time

We know that the closer we are to our goal, the less sense it makes to take great risks with our money. Shorter time frames, then, would suggest less volatile investments. If you're looking for a place to put money you're saving for a down payment on your house, it doesn't make much sense to invest in something that might fluctuate up and down (experience volatility) over a short time frame. If you're close to retiring, perhaps within five years, you are better off in less risky, less volatile investments. A short window of time to work within means you can't really afford any major downswing in your investment that may happen over that short period.

Cost of Goal

It's all relative. Depending upon how much you think a goal will cost, relative to your ability to put money aside to pay for the goal, you may want to invest more aggressively or choose a more conservative approach. In other words, if you need $10,000 in a certain amount of time, but you can only afford to put away a small amount at a time, you may choose more aggressive, higher return, types of investments. If you can put much more money away to meet that $10,000 goal, you can afford to choose more conservative, lower expected return types of investments. The bar below points out which investments are generally considered more aggressive and which more conservative.

Investment Performance

If you are a thrill seeker and you like the idea of investing for maximum growth, then you may very well choose to invest in the most aggressive investments available. If you prefer a steady-as-she-goes kind of approach, a more conservative strategy will feel right.

Investment Risk

From a more technical perspective, there is the additional factor of investment risk. This is simply the increased possibility of losing some of your investment to volatility. As we've said before, return and risk are tied together. By trying to achieve a certain return on your investments to meet your goals, you must assume the relative risk associated with those returns. And the converse, if you are comfortable at higher or lower risk levels, that comfort will dictate which return categories you are likely to fall into. Remember, everything is relative in the investment business when it comes to risk and return.

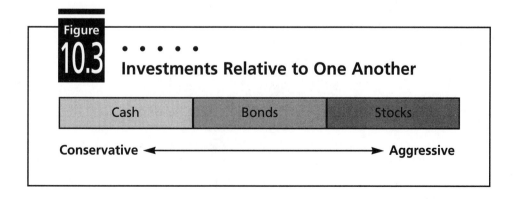

Figure 10.3

Investments Relative to One Another

| Cash | Bonds | Stocks |

Conservative ◄─────────────────► Aggressive

Doing the Math: Asset Allocation

Although asset allocation is often presented as somewhat magical, you can certainly calculate for yourself how different allocations might perform over time, based on historical investment performance data. In Chapter 12, we'll do an exercise so you can see how the investments you have already selected are working for you—or what changes might be in order.

Putting It Together
Building a Portfolio

Your portfolio is all of the different investments and things of value that you own. As adults, many of us have deliberately created portfolios, or perhaps we've simply collected a group of unrelated investments. Many people have not begun the process of being specific about the investments they select for themselves. Whatever your starting point, it's always appropriate to evaluate your current approach to investing and see if changes are in order. If you have a portfolio that was not built deliberately, it may need some fine tuning to be able to help you meet your long-term financial goals.

Let's begin the process of mapping out your portfolio by taking a look at some generic portfolios and how they each might help investors meet specific investment needs. Then we'll take a look at your portfolio, or portfolios, and see if any adjustments are in order.

What Do Portfolios Look Like?

Most of the time, portfolios are shown using pie charts like the ones shown in Figure 11.1, with individual slices representing the different investments individuals select for their portfolios. This is one of the easiest ways to

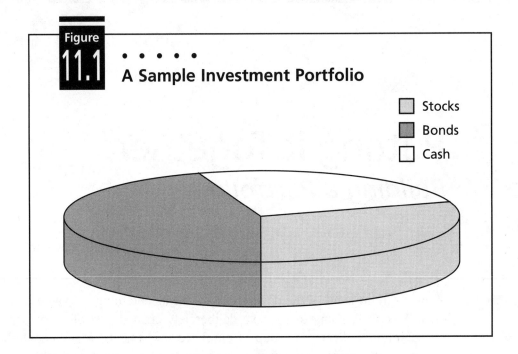

Figure 11.1

• • • • •
A Sample Investment Portfolio

☐ Stocks
■ Bonds
☐ Cash

visualize how much of each kind of asset you've selected and to see their weighting relative to each other.

Your "Big Picture" Portfolio and Individual Goal Portfolios

There are really two ways to allocate investments, and ideally, you should do both.

The first way is the simplest, and that is to look at all of your investments together, relative to your most significant goals and objectives and feelings about risk taking. The second way takes a bit more time because it involves looking at each of your financial goals individually to be sure that your investments are structured in a way that will help you meet your long-term objectives.

Before we get started evaluating your asset allocation choices, let's talk about some of the different issues that come up when you begin the process of thinking about making investment decisions.

Investment Goal, Time Frame, and Asset Allocation Worksheet

Investment Goal and Time Frame	Asset Allocation	Comments
House purchase, two years	100% Cash	Because this money needs to be safe more than it needs to grow, it should stay invested in cash.
College education, 10 years	50% fixed income, 40% large company stock, 10% cash	Because ten years is long enough to ride out some bumps in the stock market, almost half is invested in stocks. The remainder is invested in bonds that will generate income and perhaps increase in value.
College education, three years	75% cash, 25% short-term bonds	At this point, safety is the watchword because this money will be used very shortly. Most of this money is in cash, and the remainder is in the least volatile category of bonds.
Vacation home, 20 years	75% stocks, 25% long-term bonds	Because this is a "wish-list" item, and because the time frame is fairly long, it makes sense to try to grow this money as much as possible over the expected time frame. To cushion the volatility of the stock market, a good portion of this portfolio is invested in long-term bonds. *(continued)*

Investment Goal and Time Frame	Asset Allocation	Comments
House addition, six years	100% intermediate-term bonds	In this case, the time frame for meeting the goal is short, so a conservative allocation investment in intermediate-term bonds makes a lot of sense.
Retirement, five years	50% stocks, 50% bonds	Because this retiree wants to continue growing her money even during the early years of a retirement that could last up to 30 years, she's chosen to invest fairly aggressively.
Retirement, 20 years	80% stocks (heavily weighted toward aggressive funds), 20% long-term bonds	The goal here is to accumuate as much money as possible, with little concern about risk. Stocks, and aggressive ones at that, are a good choice.
Income, 30 years (a retired person)	80% bonds with varied maturities, 20% cash	Because the goal here is to generate income over a long period of time, the idea of investing in bonds or bond funds that have different maturities makes the most sense. Keeping some cash on hand for emergencies is also smart.

Investment Choices for Younger Investors

The primary challenge for younger investors is usually finding the money to invest in the first place. Having said that, it's important to note that many younger people today recognize the importance of long-term financial planning. We often hear young people talk about the fragility of the Social Security system and their interest in financial independence. The best place to start is to work hard to squeeze some investment money out of the monthly budget and focus on developing a portfolio of investments targeted toward a long-term financial plan.

A good place to start is with cash. While this doesn't sound like a very strategic move, the first step in the investment process is to develop a cash "cushion" so if things get difficult financially for any reason, you won't have to cannibalize the less-liquid investments to cover short-term bills. Once that base is covered, you might want to take a look at investing in stock mutual funds for long-range goals. These will get your feet wet and will give your money some long-term growth opportunities. If you're focusing on any short-term investment goals at this point, like a real estate down payment, keep that money separate, in a less risky investment.

Investment Choices for Mid-Life Investors

You've achieved some of your financial goals, in all likelihood, at this point, and you may very well be on your way toward achieving many more.

High Income/High Expenses

Lots of people reach midlife and have the highest levels of income and expenses at the same time, making increasing the amounts of money they save and invest fairly difficult. If this is the case for you, focus on your long-term goals first, retirement in particular, to be sure you'll do the saving and investing you need to. Although you may be faced with tapping long-term savings to meet current expenses, like college bills for the kids, be careful about reallocating your investments to a more conservative approach now; you'll need some growth over time, too.

Capital Preservation or Growth

At this stage of the game, with initial asset gathering behind you and retirement in sight, the natural tension between wanting to preserve capital you've accumulated and needing continued growth of your assets begins to make itself known. As we've said before, you'll need to balance all of the key elements of your investment decision-making picture—time, goals, comfort with risks, and the investments themselves—to be sure you make decisions that are both technically sound and personally comfortable.

Investment Choices for Retirement Investors

How you choose to invest your retirement assets has an awful lot to do with the kind of income you'll need to generate from those investments. If income sources like Social Security and company pensions will cover the bulk of your expenses, you can continue to focus on investing for growth. If you need to generate an income stream from your investments, invest more heavily in bonds and stocks that can generate income, and focus on preserving your capital. Take a second look at your retirement income and expenses worksheets in Chapter 2—they'll help you know where your income is coming from and how you'll need to invest your retirement assets.

Five Years Before Retirement

At this stage, you still need and want growth in your retirement investment portfolio, so some exposure to stocks or equity investments is necessary. But because you'll be needing some of this money within a fairly short time frame, it's important that a good chunk of it is invested for stability and income. As you move even closer to retirement, you may want to decrease your investment in stocks or stock funds in favor of fixed-income investments or cash.

Early Years of Retirement

Depending on how long you expect your retirement to last, you may want to focus some attention on stocks. Length of retirement is especially important for early retirees to think about. Be sure to pick investments that offer some relative stability. This is not the time to experiment with "hot" stocks. If you are using the income from your portfolio to live on, you'll probably be looking at investing the bulk of your assets in fixed-income selections, either taxable or tax-advantaged, and keeping some assets very liquid as well.

Later Retirement

At this point, the primary investment goal is most often generation of income and access to cash for unforeseen expenses. If you have a large portfolio and relatively low income needs, it may be prudent to keep a small portion of your assets exposed to investments that offer long-term growth.

Where You Are Now

Your Investment Portfolio Today

Through the process of saving and investing money in different places for different investment goals, you have already created a personal investment portfolio. This chapter will help you to identify where you are now and what each of the specific investments in your portfolio are. It will also help you to determine what changes to make in order to achieve long-term financial and personal investment goals.

On Your Things of Value Worksheet, or on a separate piece of paper, list all of the investments and things of value that you own. For purposes of this exercise, include even those things that you do not specifically consider retirement savings or investments. List everything that has value that you could sell for cash. For example, the equity in your home (the part you own and not the bank's portion), cars, furniture, bank accounts, vacation homes, and jewelry. Write down the dollar value of each investment or item (you might have to estimate market value on nondollar items). If your investments are stocks, bonds, or cash, note that too. Be sure not to overlook any retirement or other savings accounts that you have but have not contributed to in a long time.

Now, add up the total value of all of your investments. Keep in mind the difference between the type of account holding your investments—401(k), IRA, annuity, Keogh, etc., and the investments themselves inside the accounts— individual stocks and bonds, mutual funds, CDs, etc. Record the individual

Your Things of Value Worksheet

Categories of Investments	The Dollar Value of Your Valuables
Stocks	
Stock funds	
Bonds	
Bond funds	
Cash	
CDs	
Equity in your home	
Cars	
Recreational vehicle(s)	
Home furnishings	
Jewelry	
Collections	
Life insurance (cash value)	
Other investments	
Other assets	
Total	

	Figure 12.1 • • • • • Sample Investor's Chart		
Account	**Dollar Value**	**Percentage of Total Portfolio**
Cash or Money Market Accounts	$ 6,000	15%
Bond Funds	$ 8,000	20%
Real Estate (Home equity)	$12,000	30%
Stocks	$14,000	35%
Total	**$40,000**	**100%**

investments, not the accounts holding them. See the Sample Investor's Chart in Figure 12.1.

This gives you the information you need to create a pie chart of your personal investment portfolio. See Figure 12.2 for an example of a pie chart. Before you can make good decisions about the changes that are in order, you need to have a clear picture of where you are! Using the worksheet below, draw your portfolio pie chart using the information from Your Things of Value Worksheet. To fill in the pie, take each of your investment subtotals and divide by the total of all of your investments. Do this for each category. This calculation gives you the percentage of your portfolio that each type of investment represents. After you determine the amounts, draw pie slices that proportionately represent the different percentages.

Asset Allocation and Investment Returns

The goal of this process is to allocate your investments so that you have the right mix of risk and return to achieve your goals in the time frames you have set. In order to be sure that that will happen, you'll need to do some math

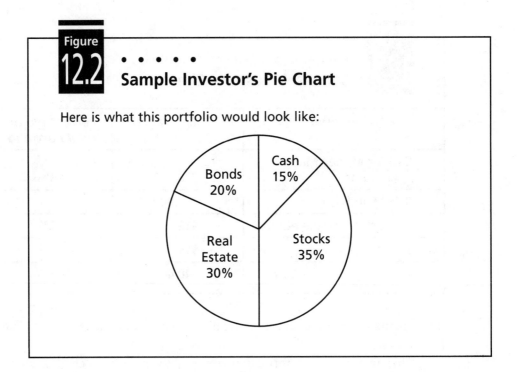

Figure 12.2

• • • • •

Sample Investor's Pie Chart

Here is what this portfolio would look like:

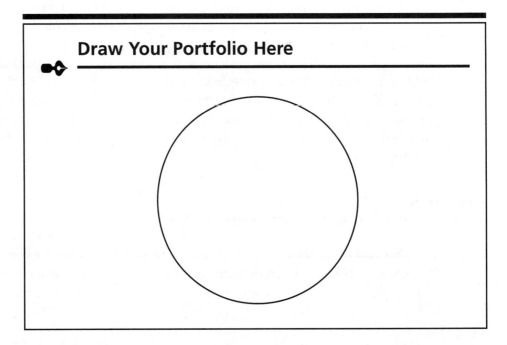

Draw Your Portfolio Here

(we'll make it simple, we promise) to see if the investments you have chosen will work best.

To do this, you'll use actual investment performance information or make assumptions about historical investment performance. If, when you do the math, the results indicate that the investments you have chosen will not get you to where you'd like to be, you may need to change your investment allocations.

Let's talk about the process of estimating investment returns for a portfolio, so you'll know how to do the math yourself. To start, you'll need to know how much of each type of investment you have selected, and you'll need information about the return that investment has generated, over as long a period of time as the returns have been tracked.

Here's an explanation of how these calculations work, and an example. The six steps are:

Step 1. Decide whether you are calculating your overall portfolio returns, or if you are looking separately at investments for individual goals.

Step 2. Using the information from step 1, fill in the Calculating Your Own Portfolio Returns Worksheet. List each asset by name, dollar value, and the percentage of your total portfolio that each item represents.

Step 3. Now, fill in column 4, expected return, for each investment you've listed. Search quarterly statements or other investment firm information to discover this number. If you don't have this information at hand, or if you have it for just one or two years, use the historical investment performance information in Chapter 6 instead.

Step 4. Here is where you see how the return each investment is earning impacts your bottom line. Grab a calculator or pencil and paper, and multiply the expected return for each investment by the percentage of your portfolio that investment makes up. In our example, stocks make up 30 percent of the total portfolio, and their expected annual return is 10 percent. Multiply 30 percent (0.3 on a calculator) by 10 (.01), then multiply by 100, and you get 3 percent. This 3 percent is the amount of return that the stock portion of the portfolio contributes to your whole investment portfolio. Do this for each investment.

Step 5. The final step in the process of calculating your expected portfolio return is to add up the numbers in column 5. This number is the percentage return your portfolio can be reasonably expected to deliver to you.

Step 6. To find out the annual dollar value of the return you are earning, multiply all of the money in your portfolio, (the total in column 2), by the expected portfolio return (the total in column 5).

At this point, you have the information you need to decide if you need to move your investments around to earn the return that will allow you to meet your goals. Maybe the number you've calculated comes out right where you need it to be. More commonly, you'll want, or need, to make some changes to get you where you expect to be. Another way to confirm that you're on the right track is to take a quick look at the Achieving Financial Goals Worksheet in Chapter 2 to be sure that you're contributing as much as you need to reach your goals.

In Figure 12.3, we can see that this portfolio of $10,000 can be expected to earn 6.2 percent per year, on average. To find out how much money a 6.2 percent return will generate, grab the nearest pocket calculator and multiply $10,000 by 6.2 percent ($\times$ .062). The result? About $620 per year in growth. As you can see from the example, the amounts of investments earning higher or lower rates can significantly impact your bottom line.

If the dollar growth you calculate is not what you need to reach your investment goals, make some changes, for example, increasing the level of risk you're taking in order to generate some additional return. If you're right on track, congratulations are in order! If it looks like you'll meet your goals with money to spare, you may want to increase the level of "safety" in your overall portfolio, or set some other goals to achieve.

Figure 12.3 • • • • •
Calculating Portfolio Returns

1. Asset	2. Dollar Value	3. Percent of Total Portfolio	4. Expected Return*	5. Expected Portfolio Return (No. 3 x No. 4)
Stocks	$3,000	30% (0.3)	10.0% (0.1)	3.0%
Bonds	$2,000	20% (0.2)	6.0% (.06)	1.2%
Cash	$5,000	50% (0.5)	4.0% (.04)	2.0%
Total	$10,000	100%		6.2%

* These returns are samples used for this illustration. They do not reflect actual returns on any "real" portfolio(s).

Calculating Your Own Portfolio Returns Worksheet

1. Asset	2. Dollar Value	3. Percent of Total Portfolio	4. Expected Dollar Return	5. Expected Portfolio Return (No. 3 x No. 4)
Total		**100%**		

Note: You may want to make copies of this page, so you can do the math for new goals, and evaluate whether any changes to your asset allocation—or investments chosen to meet individual goals—are in order, on a regular basis.

Double Your Money!

You may have heard about the "Rule of 72." It has nothing to do with your 72nd birthday but everything to do with easily figuring how fast your money will grow at different rates of return. Here's how it works: Take the number 72 and divide it by the percentage your investment will probably grow in any one year. An investment like a small company stock fund might grow at 12 percent in a good year, so if we divide 72 by 12, we get 6. The result (6) is the number of years it will take for the money in that particular investment to double under compounded interest. An investment that grows at 6 percent a year will double in 12 years. You get the idea. It helps to have this information, too, as you try to balance amount of money and time frame factors to meet your goals.

Asset Allocation Alternatives

Let's take a look at how a couple different asset allocation models perform over time. Let's keep it simple by looking at just three alternatives. You can learn how to do the math from our example in Figure 12.4 and calculate as many complex asset allocations as you'd like.

Over most of the last century investment performance has been in the range of 10 percent for stocks and 5 percent for bonds. So we'll use those numbers to make some educated guesses about future performance as well.

Grab a calculator or pencil and paper, and multiply the expected return for each investment by the percentage of the asset allocation portfolio example that each investment makes up. In Portfolio One, stocks make up 50 percent of the total portfolio and their expected return is 10 percent. Multiply 50 percent (0.5 on a calculator) by 10 (0.1), then multiply by 100, and you get 5 percent. This 5 percent is the amount of return that the stock portion of the portfolio contributes to your whole investment portfolio. Do the same calculation for the bonds portion of the portfolio, using an expected return of 5 percent. Add the two numbers together. The result is the annual return you can expect for that sample portfolio. Do this for each sample asset allocation you'd like to see played out.

Here are the annual returns, using this approach, for our three sample portfolios.

Figure 12.4 Figuring Expected Returns for Various Asset Allocations		
Portfolio One	*Portfolio Two*	*Portfolio Three*
Stocks 50% Bonds 50%	Stocks 75% Bonds 25%	Stocks 25% Bonds 75%
Average annual return: 7.5%	Average annual return: 8.75%	Average annual return: 6.25%

The final step is to translate these numbers back into your formula for reaching your investment goals. To do that, take a look at the compounding guide in Figure 12.5.

In our example, we've assumed that we're starting with a pot of $1,000 and that you don't add to it over time. So this chart shows the effects of annual compounding on your initial investment. If you want to know very roughly what these returns look like for larger numbers, just add a zero and move the decimal point right one space for each increment of $10,000 you add. So for a $10,000 investment held 15 years that earns 6.25 percent annually, you'd have approximately $24,820.

Figure 12.5 **Effects of Annual Compounding**

Rate of Return	5 Years	10 Years	15 Years	20 Years	25 Years	30 Years
6.25%	$1,354	$1,833	$2,482	$3,361	$4,552	$6,164
7.50%	$1,435	$2,061	$2,958	$4,247	$6,098	$8,754
8.75%	$1,521	$2,313	$3,519	$5,352	$8,142	$12,384

Following Your Plan

Now that you've completed the process of developing an asset allocation plan, you've already made a number of financial and investment decisions. The final decisions involve picking specific investments for your investment accounts, and deciding whether or not an investment adviser makes sense for you, both of which we'll cover in Part Four.

At this point, we'd like to stop, take a breath, and point out a couple of important things. What you have done here is to create a financial "road map" for yourself. You have a plan to follow, a strategy, a framework for making the individual investment decisions we're all confronted with regularly.

Because your plan implements diversification and asset allocation, your portfolio should be able to withstand day-to-day volatility of the investment markets, and even some hiccups in the investment performance of the individual investments you've chosen. You have taken the appropriate steps to both cushion the blow of any investment down drafts, and take advantage of wonderful upswings, too. This should take some of the fear out of worrying about conflicting predictions of investment experts. Try not to fall into the trap of moving your money around as a result of what pundits are saying. If you find yourself falling into that mental trap, revisit Part Two and rethink your perspective on risk. Making some asset allocation changes also may be in order.

Which is not to say you don't need to take inventory of your investment plan periodically—you absolutely do! We'd like to suggest a framework for revisiting your investments, a schedule for reviewing where you are and where you need to go. Let's start with what *not* to do. When you sign up for a diet program, you usually weigh in only once a week. Why? Because more frequent check-ins don't tell the story of a trend. What you weigh one day or the next may actually be misleading. What matters is the trend over time. In the world of investing, up-to-the-minute information is available. Moment-by-moment information, though, doesn't show you a trend. The problem is that making investment decisions as frequently as the information is available is as reckless as never reviewing your investments at all.

So how often is often enough? Figure 12.6 shows a schedule that is both reasonable and takes into account changes that people experience. From the date you began your financial planning process, schedule a "review" of your plan six months in the future. At that point, unless there have been some sig-

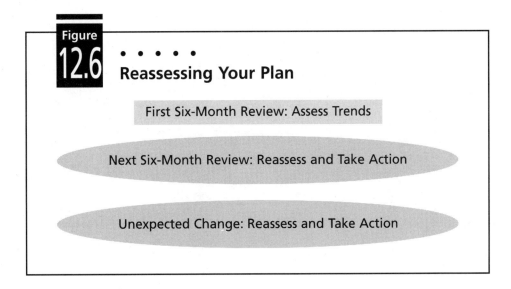

Figure 12.6

• • • • •
Reassessing Your Plan

First Six-Month Review: Assess Trends

Next Six-Month Review: Reassess and Take Action

Unexpected Change: Reassess and Take Action

nificant changes in your life or goals that prompt some financial changes, just review the trends. What does that mean? Take a look at the decisions you've made and the asset allocation(s) you've put together. Is there anything you're rethinking? Any choice that "bugs" you? Something new you're mulling over? This is the time to simply make a note about changes you're considering. If you can, gather any information that is relevant to your decision.

At the next six-month mark, one year from the date you made your plan, update your assessments and take any action that seems to be in order. It is important to be as deliberate about your changes as you have been about making the plan in the first place.

And, or course, when something changes in term of your goals or financial situation, take action. Emergencies may require you to liquidate an investment or to roll over a retirement plan account. Do what you need to in response to your situation.

Six months later, reassess again. Staying on this schedule is both reasonable and achievable. Which is how investment decision making should be.

At this point, you have two options. If you're ready to move on to Part Four, Picking Investments and Professional Services, and to make some specific investment decisions for yourself, go ahead and do that. If you'd like to read a bit more detailed information about how asset allocation works the way it does, read Chapter 13 before moving on to Part Four.

How Asset Allocation Was Born

The Story of Modern Portfolio Theory

Today, the asset allocation process and financial planning incorporates "modern portfolio theory," a body of knowledge about how investments work in combination with one another. This approach measures investments in a number of different ways to come up with the best possible blend for particular investment goals.

Here is how some of these measurements work.

Correlation

Correlation coefficients measure how different investments perform in similar market conditions. Investments that are expected to do the same thing at the same time have a correlation coefficient of 1. Investments with negative correlation coefficients are expected to move in opposite directions. The lower the correlation between the two investments, the more likely it is that you can improve your overall return without adding more risk.

Beta

Beta coefficients measure the degree to which a stock's price changes in relationship to changes in the stock market as a whole. A stock with a beta of

1 moves with the market. Stocks with betas greater than 1 are more volatile, and stocks with betas less than 1 are less volatile than the market overall. So, a stock with a beta of 1.5 would show a gain of 15 percent if the market moved up 10 percent (10 percent × 1.5 = 15 percent).

Risk and Return

The potential for return or reward is directly related to risk. You cannot have one without the other. Because of this relationship, investments can be combined in different ways to create portfolios that have different levels of risk and return.

Portfolio Optimization

Portfolio optimization consists of combining different types of assets in a portfolio to give investors the highest possible return for a given level of risk, or the least amount of risk for a given level of return. Portfolio optimization is a complicated term for a fairly basic concept, again based on modern portfolio theory.

Efficient Market

Efficient market theory states that the market overall is so inherently efficient that prices change as new information becomes available. In an efficient market, a stock's price accurately reflects all of the information that is available about that security, so the level of risk in a particular security is already reflected in its market price. Therefore, outsmarting a truly efficient market is fairly difficult.

The idea of an efficient portfolio is directly related to the idea of an efficient market. In the same way that a market for securities can be efficient, a portfolio of investments can be efficient. An efficient portfolio of investments offers the highest possible reward for a given level of risk, or conversely, the least amount of risk for an expected reward.

Efficient Frontier

Although this sounds like it has something to do with the Wild West, the efficient frontier is simply a graph or picture of the risk and return balance of a particular investment portfolio. An efficient frontier chart shows where a particular mix of investments fits in the risk and return spectrum. The "frontier" is the part of the chart that shows where the best possible mixes of risk and return are located. An efficient portfolio will be very close to the efficient frontier on the chart.

Figure 13.1 shows what an efficient frontier chart looks like.

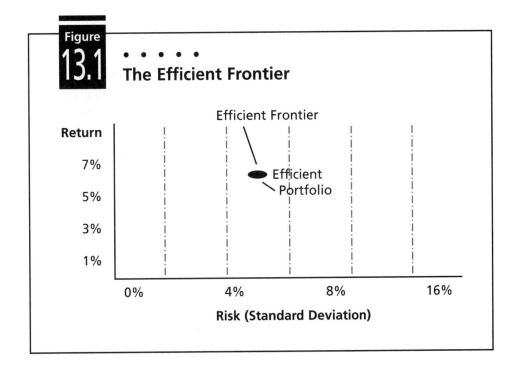

Figure **13.1**

• • • • •
The Efficient Frontier

Efficient Frontier

Return

7%   Efficient
             Portfolio
5%

3%

1%

0%   4%   8%   16%

Risk (Standard Deviation)

PART
4

Picking Investments and Professional Services

When you need a new dishwasher, you know where to go to get the information you need about which brand and model are best. You probably even have a store where you generally buy items like these, and maybe even a salesperson you trust to tell you whether the one that's on sale is really the best model they carry. When it comes to financial services and investment products, though, it's a whole different ball game. The questions are much more complicated, and the answers have many pieces.

Now that you have a clear idea of how to organize your approach to investing, and you've developed an investment strategy for yourself, the final step in the process is to establish investment accounts and select investment products and services that will enable you to achieve your investment goals. The goal of Part Four is to provide a framework for understanding available investment products and services, and give you tools to understand how they work and what you're really buying. Without oversimplifying, we'd like you to feel as comfortable about selecting and buying investment products as you do about selecting and buying appliances for your home.

Before we start, though, it's important for you to become comfortable with this very important thought: *It's your money, and ultimately, it's your decision.* It may seem as if we've harped on this a bit, but it is so important for you to believe in your own ability to make good judgments about investment products and services. No matter what anyone else tells you, there is no reason to make urgent, hurried decisions to buy investment products of any kind, and there is never any reason at all to do something with your money that makes you feel uncomfortable. We often hear about people who have lost money in one investment scheme or another, or bought products that promised glorious returns with absolutely no risk to their money. In Part Two you learned that in the investment business, if it sounds too good to be true, it is. What does this mean to your investment decision-making process? Simply that you should always take the time to understand investments you are considering. You should be able to clearly articulate to yourself the benefits—and possible risks—of the investment choices you make. Never buy any investment that involves a high-pressure sale, or one that causes your cautionary inner alarm bells to ring. If you feel "funny" about a product for any reason, *don't buy it!* With the number of excellent investment products available to investors today, compromises are rarely—if ever—called for.

14

Do It Yourself or Call In the Experts?

There are really two ways to manage your money and investments. First, you can choose to do it all yourself, everything from opening accounts and picking investments to reviewing and filing the statements away in your home office or desk. Another approach is to find someone to help you establish goals, open appropriate accounts, and select products that make the most sense. If you choose to hire expert help, you still have a responsibility to yourself to develop a basic understanding of how the investment business works. This is the best protection from practitioners who are not actually the experts you'd like them to be, or from poor decisions made by pros. One of the classic investing errors people in the industry cite is the establishment of a tax-deferred account, an individual retirement account, or IRA, for example, that holds tax-advantaged investments. This is as silly as wearing a raincoat on a sunny day, there is absolutely no reason to do it. Why? Because alone, either the IRA account or the tax-advantaged bonds offer all of the tax benefits you can realistically take advantage of. Using both together doesn't double the tax benefit. But there is no way for you to know this is a silly strategy unless you have a frame of reference for what makes good investing sense and what doesn't.

So, let's begin at the beginning, with places investors put different kinds of investments. This may sound kind of elementary, but we often are asked to clarify the differences between different types of investments, and the accounts that hold them. One source of the confusion is the names for the accounts and products. Often, they sound more like alphabet soup than consumer-friendly product labels. So here's an end to the confusion.

Figure 14.1 shows two investment accounts, each holding different types of investments. With the number of different accounts we can choose from, it's easy to see why creating an investment plan that captures all of this information can be quite complicated. In this example, we're showing an IRA and a 401(k) retirement plan account, which many investors today contribute to. (We'll talk more about all of the different kinds of accounts later in Part Four.) Within any type of investment account, you can generally select different investments that will help you reach the investment goals you have established.

Many types of investment accounts have names that describe their purpose or benefit in some way. Some, of course, are harder to translate. To simplify, we've broken the different types of accounts into two broad categories: retirement accounts and other investment accounts. Retirement accounts typically offer tax benefits for long-term, retirement-oriented savings and investing. Investment accounts can be established for any purpose you like and some offer specific tax benefits, in certain situations.

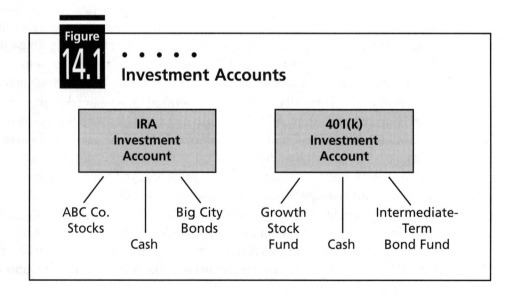

Figure 14.1 • • • • •

Investment Accounts

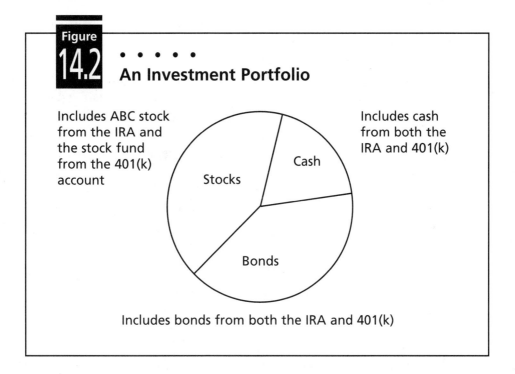

Figure 14.2 · · · · · An Investment Portfolio

Includes ABC stock from the IRA and the stock fund from the 401(k) account

Includes cash from both the IRA and 401(k)

Cash

Stocks

Bonds

Includes bonds from both the IRA and 401(k)

Figure 14.2 shows how investments in different accounts come together to make up a single investment portfolio. (See Part Three for a more complete discussion of investment portfolios.)

Tax Benefits for Investors

As we've said, retirement accounts—and some investments themselves—offer tax benefits. There are three different categories of tax benefits generally available to investors, depending on the type of investment account you establish and the types of investments selected. Here's an explanation of how these three benefits work:

1. *Tax deductible.* This means that the amount of money you put in an investment account is not taxed as income in the year that you invest it. When you make tax-deductible contributions to a 401(k) plan, for

example, the contributions can be described as pretax, meaning they are deducted from your income before federal (and in some cases, state) income taxes are calculated.

2. *Tax deferred.* Our tax system is what's called a "pay-as-you-go" system. Normally, income taxes are due when you earn income, whether it's from a job or from interest or growth in an investment account. Tax-deferred means taxes aren't due immediately, but, rather, you have the ability to pay taxes later, generally when you actually use the money.

3. *Tax free.* This is the one time when we get to break the "if it sounds too good to be true, it is" rule. This is just what you think it is: No taxes are due. For the first time, the Taxpayer Relief Act of 1997 established two kinds of tax-free investment accounts: the Roth IRA and the Education IRA (discussed in detail in Chapter 15).

Types of Accounts

Figure 14.3 shows a list of the two primary types of accounts: retirement accounts and investment accounts. It also shows the many different names these accounts have. We'll talk about each account in turn, detailing its benefits and features, and give you the information you need to know to open these accounts.

The Taxpayer Relief Act of 1997

The Taxpayer Relief Act of 1997 is a great boon for investors. This law offers investors several new types of tax-advantaged accounts, as well as a reduction in taxes owed on profits (capital gains) made by buying and holding assets that increase substantially in value over time. The tax act reduces the top capital gains rates to 20 percent for investors in the 28 percent or above tax bracket and to 10 percent for investors in the 15 percent tax bracket for investments held for more than 18 months. Rates drop again to 18 percent and 8 percent, respectively, for investments held for longer than five years, after the year 2000.

Figure 14.3 • • • • •
Chart of Accounts

Retirement Accounts (Offer tax benefits)	Investment Accounts (The growth and earnings in these accounts are taxable)
Individual Retirement Accounts • Traditional IRA • Roth IRA • Education IRA Small Business Retirement Accounts • SIMPLE 401(k)s and IRAs • SEP-IRA • Keogh Plans Employee Benefit Accounts • Defined Contribution Plan, 401(k) Plan • Tax Deferred Annuity, 403(b) Plan • Deferred Compensation Plan, 457 Plan • Thrift Plan	• Custodial (UGMA/UTMA) • Brokerage • Mutual Fund • Advisory • Trust

By reducing capital gains rates and introducing tax-free IRAs at the same time, the new tax act changes some long-held assumptions about what kinds of investments to put in which types of accounts. For years, investors had been investing in securities expected to grow at very high rates of return in tax-advantaged accounts, often to take advantage of the benefits of deferring large tax bills. With this change, investing for growth in taxable accounts can result in a very reasonable tax bill. At the same time, the benefits of investing for the long term in IRAs have increased as well, offering both tax-deferred and tax-free growth. What does all this mean? More choices about where to invest, and lower tax bills as your investments grow over time—overall, good news for investors.

Establishing Investment Accounts

The first step in putting your investment process into motion is to establish investment accounts. To do this, you simply complete an account application for a specific type of account. Within the accounts you establish, you'll have the flexibility to invest in the asset classes and products that will enable you to meet your long-term goals. As we've outlined previously, investment accounts fall into two general categories:

1. Retirement accounts.
2. Other investment accounts.

We'll talk about both kinds of accounts, but we'll begin with retirement investment accounts, available to all investors in one form or another. Retirement investing has become increasingly important as the responsibility for providing pensions has moved from companies to individuals. Today, lots of people participate in company-sponsored retirement plans, and many are also active retirement investors through IRAs and other investment accounts. Today, most of us are responsible for creating our own retirement security.

There are three types of retirement accounts:

1. A retirement account you establish for yourself, outside of your employment or work situation.
2. Retirement accounts for self-employed individuals and small businesses.
3. Retirement plans offered by employers to their employees.

Accounts in the second and third category are offered only to employees. The choices you have about retirement accounts include whether or not to participate in the plan, how much to contribute, and how to allocate your money among the investment options in the plan. These accounts (with one exception we'll talk about shortly) all have one important thing in common; they are established specifically for the purpose of investing for retirement. Typically with these accounts investors do have access to their money in certain situations other than retirement, although penalties and taxes may be due.

For most people, it makes excellent sense to participate up to the maximum allowed limits in employee benefit plans offered to you. Generally, contributions to these plans are taken out of your paycheck, making participation very easy. The contribution limits on these plans are much higher than the limits on IRAs, meaning the tax benefits are bigger. For everyone who qualifies to take advantage of it, the don't-miss investment account has to be the new Roth IRA. You just can't beat tax-free returns, and while making contributions to a Roth IRA won't reduce your current tax bill, it certainly is the best deal for most investors for the long haul.

We'll explain how these accounts work, their tax benefits, and their value and limitations to you as an investor. Remember that for each of these accounts, with only a few exceptions, you make the decisions about which investments to put in the accounts, and you decide how much of each type of investment makes the most sense for you.

Establishing Your Individual Retirement Investment Account

You have a number of choices and options about the types of retirement accounts available to you. What options make the most sense depends on your individual situation. Take the time to learn about your choices. When it comes to examining the tax issues with some of these accounts, you may want to consult a tax professional.

Individual Retirement Accounts (IRAs)*

This category of account is available to everyone with earned income, regardless of the benefits offered through one's employers. Every year, each of us is eligible to contribute $2,000 to whatever combination of traditional and Roth IRAs we choose. Education IRAs are not included in this $2,000 limit. What will be different for each of us is our ability to deduct traditional IRA contributions from our current year's tax bill. This is because the tax deduc-

---

*Because the income limits and phaseouts change so often, for every type of account we talk about, we recommend consulting with an accountant or other tax adviser for more detailed information about how the IRA income limits and rules apply to your specific situation. Information here should not be construed as advice.

tibility of traditional IRAs is limited by one's level of income; the more you (and your spouse) earn, the less of your traditional IRA contribution is deductible. Traditional IRAs are not deductible at all for high earners unless they lack access to qualified retirement plans sponsored by their employers. The maximum annual IRA contribution for an individual is $2,000, and $4,000 for married couples. This amount may be split between Roth and traditional IRAs. You choose the investments for the account for either type of IRA. You can open IRAs through banks and investment firms. We'll talk about how to do that in Chapter 16.

Traditional Individual Retirement Accounts (IRAs)

The traditional IRA is familiar to many investors, some of whom can make contributions on a tax-deductible basis. As incomes increase, though, the ability to make tax-deductible contributions to a traditional IRA decreases. Whether or not your contributions are tax deductible, all of the earnings and growth in traditional IRAs are tax deferred. At retirement, IRA withdrawals are taxed as ordinary income. If you withdraw IRA assets early (before age 59½) you may be subject to a 10 percent IRS penalty. You can use money accumulated in a traditional IRA for retirement, of course, and up to $10,000 (a lifetime maximum) can be used for a first-time home purchase. Investors also have the ability to use traditional IRA assets for qualified higher education expenses without penalty. These accounts can be established whether you work for someone else, are self-employed, or have earned income from a hobby. However, total contributions cannot exceed earned income. The deductibility of contributions for traditional IRAs is reduced as incomes increase. Over the next ten years, the phaseout ranges will be between $50,000 and $60,000 for single filers, and $80,000 to $100,000 for married couples filing jointly. Importantly, you can now establish an IRA even if your spouse is covered by an employer's retirement plan.

Roth IRA

The Roth IRA was established by the Taxpayer Relief Act of 1997. Contributions to Roth IRAs are made with after-tax dollars, but all growth in the account takes place on a tax-free basis. Importantly, these IRAs will grow at the same rate a traditional IRA does, but at withdrawal, for investors age 59½ and older whose accounts have been open for five years or more, no taxes will be due on income received from the Roth IRA account. Unlike traditional IRAs, investors can contribute to Roth IRAs even after they reach age 70½. The amount of contributions to Roth IRAs is reduced as adjusted gross income (AGI) increases from $150,000 to $160,000 for married couples filing jointly, and $95,000 to $110,000 for single filers.

Education IRA

Also established by the Taxpayer Relief Act of 1997, education IRAs allow taxpayers to set aside up to $500 per year in an account earmarked for a minor's education. If the money in the account isn't used for educational purposes by the time the minor turns 30, the money can be transferred to another child in the same family. The contribution limit is phased out as AGI increases from $95,000 to $110,000.

Rollover IRAs

Also called "conduit" IRAs, this is the type of account to establish if you are leaving a job or retiring, and are eligible for a distribution from a retirement plan. This is a traditional IRA account, but it includes information that the money within came from another qualified plan. This is important in case you move to a new employer and want to transfer the money back into a new qualified plan there. In order to avoid having 20 percent of your account balance withheld in the form of taxes—and if you're under age 59½, getting hit with a 10 percent early withdrawal penalty—you need to have your retirement plan money transferred directly into an IRA rollover account.

Should You Convert to a Roth IRA?

Investors with traditional IRAs and AGIs under $100,000 (single or married) have the option to convert traditional IRA accounts to a Roth IRA. This may be a good idea if you think you'll be in a high tax bracket when you re-tire, and you want to take advantage of tax-free withdrawals at retirement. You will pay income taxes on the amounts you convert. Special tax treatment is available to investors who convert to a Roth before the end of 1998.

Figure 15.1 shows the timing of taxes paid on the three different types of IRAs available to investors.

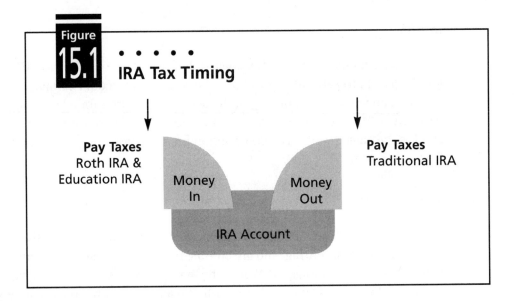

Figure 15.1 IRA Tax Timing

Pay Taxes
Roth IRA &
Education IRA

Money In

Money Out

IRA Account

Pay Taxes
Traditional IRA

Establishing Other Types of Retirement and Investment Accounts

Ready for more choices? We hope so. Individual retirement accounts are just one of your options; you have lots of alternatives when it comes to structuring the accounts that house your investments. Some of these choices are offered by employers, and some you open yourself, either through an investment professional or directly with a financial institution.

A Word about Annuities

Sold by insurance agents, brokers, and other financial professionals, annuities are a hybrid product. Part insurance contract, part mutual fund, and part investment account, they offer several unique features. Variable annuities allow you to invest in subaccounts (which are similar to, and often run just like, mutual funds) to expose your money to the growth that the stock market and other investment options offer. Variable annuities also offer a death benefit, which sounds kind of gloomy, but offers investors a guarantee that their beneficiaries will receive all of the money they invest in a variable annuity, even if the market has done poorly. Fixed annuities offer a guaranteed or fixed rate of return, something the stock and bond markets don't. All annuities offer investors the ability to "annuitize," i.e., to turn the value of the account into a series of payments that can last the lifetime of the person who owns the annuity and/or someone else they specify. All of these goodies come at a cost, of course, making the fees on many annuities rather steep, especially compared with mutual funds. For some investors, though, they make a lot of sense.

If you are considering purchasing an annuity, ask to see the contract. Ask about (and look in the contract for) things like:

- "Teaser" rates of interest on the fixed accounts (These are higher rates that are offered for a limited period of time.)
- Surrender charges (like back-end loads on a mutual fund which can be up to 7 or 8 percent) (Back-end loads are sales charges applied when an investor sells an investment.)
- Access to your money—often you can take out as much as 10 percent per year
- Availability of your money—without surrender charges—under certain adverse circumstances, like terminal illness, divorce, etc.
- Although insurance is a component of an annuity, if you are only looking for insurance, you may very well be better off with a term life policy which is much less expensive

What Is My Plan Qualified to Do?

All of the retirement plans we're going to talk about below are called "qualified" plans. This doesn't mean that they are qualified to do anything in particular. In this case, it simply means that they qualify for certain tax benefits. So why don't they just say that, you wonder? We wonder, too.

Small Business Retirement Accounts

If you own a small business, these are the types of plans you may be offering now, or that you might want to consider offering, to your employees. If you work for a small business, these are the types of retirement savings and investment plans you might have available to you. With each of these accounts, you can select how much of each type of the investment options in the plan to invest in. Employers generally select a family or group of investments to include in these plans. If that is the case, you will simply make your selections from among this group.

SIMPLE IRAs and 401(k)s

SIMPLE stands for "savings incentive match plan for employees." The idea behind these plans is to make it easy for businesses with fewer than one hundred employees to offer retirement savings plans to their employees, and to avoid some of the paperwork and expense that often goes along with providing employee pension plans. These plans allow employees to decide how much to contribute on a pretax (tax deductible) basis and require employers to make matching contributions as well. The SIMPLE IRA and 401(k) plans are almost identical in terms of their benefits to investors. The SIMPLE 401(k) does require employers to contribute a higher match, 3 percent of salary whereas the IRA match will be between 1 percent and 3 percent of salary. For both plans, the maximum employee contribution is pegged at $6,000 for 1998. Distributions from these plans are generally taxed as ordinary income.

Simplified Employee Pensions (SEPs)

These plans are structured as individual retirement accounts or individual retirement annuities. Employers make tax-deductible contributions to these accounts. The maximum contribution to these accounts for 1998 is 15 percent of an employee's compensation or $30,000, whichever is lower.

Keogh Plans

Keogh plans are maintained by self-employed people who are either sole proprietors or partners. Interestingly, S corporation shareholders are not self-employed, according to the IRS, and so cannot establish Keogh plans. Many small businesses are incorporated as subchapter S corporations. The total contribution limits for Keogh plans for 1998 are the same that apply to corporate plans, generally the lesser of $30,000 or a percentage of net earnings.

Employee Benefit Retirement Accounts

When you participate in an employee benefit retirement plan, an account with your name on it is established. These plans generally offer tax deductibility of contributions as well as automatic payroll deductions, making them one of the easiest ways to stick to your long-term saving and investing plan. All of these plans fall into the category of defined contribution plans, meaning that the amount contributed to the plan is defined by the investor. You may have heard about defined benefit plans; these are the traditional types of pension plans offered by large companies to their employees. In a defined benefit plan, employers make contributions to the plan and manage the investment decisions for those contributions. The employer guarantees the employees a certain level of income at their retirement, usually based on years of service and highest earning levels. Employees have no control over how much money gets contributed to a defined benefit plan, nor can they make decisions about which investments the plan should choose. The money is not segregated into individual employee accounts, like in a defined contribution plan but rather is invested as one big portfolio. From calculations provided by actuaries and other financial experts, the company knows how much it needs to contribute to meet its obligations to employees' pensions. Although many small- to mid-sized companies have phased out defined benefit plans, or never established them to begin with, many large companies still offer them to their employees.

401(k) Plan

401(k)s are hands-down the most popular retirement plan of our era. They offer many important advantages such as fairly high contribution limits set by the government that are indexed to inflation ($10,000 in 1998). There may be lower limits imposed by your company, however. Current contributions to 401(k) plans are tax deductible, and growth in the account is tax deferred until retirement. All of the money you contribute to the plan is yours, always. Many employers match some, or all, of their employees' contributions, which can really add up. Some employers even make profit-sharing contributions to their company's 401(k) plans. If you have one at work, make sure to take a close look.

Tax-Sheltered Annuities, or 403(b) Plans

These plans are very similar to 401(k) plans, but they are offered only to employees of education, research institutions, and not-for-profit organizations. The annual contribution limits are the same as the limits for 401(k) plans.

Deferred Compensation Plans, or 457 Plans

Similar to 401(k) plans, these plans allow government employees to defer some of their compensation into a retirement plan. Employees can defer the lesser of $8,000 or 25 percent of compensation from taxation. These plans give people the opportunity to select the investments they choose from a larger group selected by their employer. These plans are a little different from other defined contribution plans because federal tax law requires that the money you defer remains the property of your employer until it is paid out to you.

Thrift Plans, Money Purchase Plans, Profit-Sharing Plans, and Employee Stock Plans*

Each of these plans is a different type of employee benefit program. If you have one of these types of plans available to you, and you choose to participate, an account will be established in your name. Each of these plans works in a different way, so be sure to read the materials you receive from your employer about the program.

Investment Accounts

Retirement accounts are, of course, not the only type of investment account available to you. You can open investment accounts at banks, brokerages, mutual fund companies, and investment firms. You can open accounts for your-

---

Note: This information is included as a guideline only. It should not be viewed as tax advice. Because the rules and contribution limits change quickly, please consult with your tax adviser for information specific to your personal situation.

self or for your children, or to distribute money to a charity. Businesses can have investment accounts, too. You may choose to open separate accounts for each of your investment goals, or you might prefer to open individual investment accounts for different kinds of assets. Before you start opening lots of accounts at different financial institutions, be aware of the amount of additional paperwork and fees that a large number of investment accounts can generate. You don't want to become overwhelmed with information and paperwork—you need to be able to take the time to review your investments and to make sure you are on track toward your goals.

We're all familiar with bank accounts as a place to hold cash. Banks also can establish trust accounts, which means that they have fiduciary responsibility for managing the money in an account. Banks also offer private banking services to customers with very large account balances. If you're lucky enough to have lots of money in the bank, ask about private banking. Trust accounts can be a good way to manage money for someone else—a child, or an aging parent.

Custodial accounts allow money set aside for children to be taxed at a child's lower tax rate. The money in a custodial account belongs to the child and will become hers or his at the age of legal majority in the state she or he resides. Custodial accounts are established under the Uniform Gifts/Transfers to Minors Act, often referred to as UGMA/UTMA.

Brokerage accounts can be set up at full-service national or regional firms or at discount brokers. These accounts can be set up to trade individual stocks and bonds or to hold mutual funds.

When you invest in a mutual fund, you establish a mutual fund account. If you buy more than one mutual fund from a mutual fund company it will be held in one account unless you open another account (IRA, custodial, etc.) to hold the investment.

Investment advisory accounts are established with investment advisers who manage money for you. Your relationship is with your investment adviser. For regulatory reasons, your money is held in a bank or brokerage account, and the investment adviser you have selected makes decisions about investments in the account.

Beneficiaries

When you establish an investment account, you will be asked to designate one or more beneficiaries for the account. These are persons to whom the value of your account will be given to in case something happens to you. Be sure to review this information regularly to reflect changes in your life and relationships.

Fiduciary Responsibility

Big words, but important ones. In general terms, fiduciary responsibility is the responsibility a financial institution or investment professional has to act in the best interests of their client. Banks have it when they act as trustees, and investment managers have it when they select investments for a particular investor or account. Stockbrokers, financial planners, and other investment pros have it as well. It simply means that they must have your best interests—not theirs—in mind when making decisions about your money.

Buying Investment Products
A Focus on Mutual Funds

In general, there are two primary ways to buy securities products: as individual securities and as managed products. Managed products include mutual funds, annuities, unit trusts, limited partnerships, etc. The broad category of managed products includes any type of investment that pools investors' monies and selects individual securities in which to invest. Individual securities are individual stocks and bonds and other investments. Because there is so much information available about selecting securities, we do not go into detail here on that topic.

We'll talk first about mutual funds and then about other types of managed products.

Mutual Funds: What They Are and How They Work

There are more than 6,800 mutual funds available today. Mutual funds have become the investment workhorse for many people and the way most Americans invest today. Because that is the case, we have included information you need to know to make good, comfortable decisions about mutual funds.

When you invest in a mutual fund, you are actually buying shares of ownership in an investment company. This may be the first time you've received this nugget of information, but we think it's very important to understand what you actually own when you buy mutual fund shares. An investment company, in this context, is not the same thing as a firm that invests peoples' monies on their behalf although it certainly sounds as if that should be the case. An investment company is simply the form of organization for mutual funds. The mutual fund then invests your money, and money from lots of other people, in stocks, bonds, or other kinds of investments. You, along with the other investors in the mutual fund, own shares of the mutual fund and therefore of the total pool of investments the mutual fund owns. Figure 17.1 will help you visualize what we're talking about.

The mutual fund, or investment company, actually takes the "pool" of money from investors and buys individual securities with it. Figure 17.2 shows how a stock mutual fund works. A fund's "portfolio" includes all of the securities it buys.

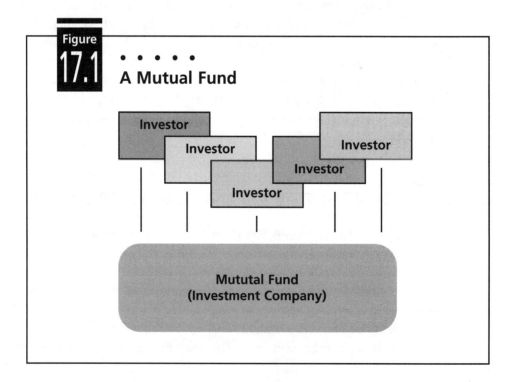

Figure 17.1

• • • • •
A Mutual Fund

Investor
Investor
Investor
Investor
Investor

Mututal Fund
(Investment Company)

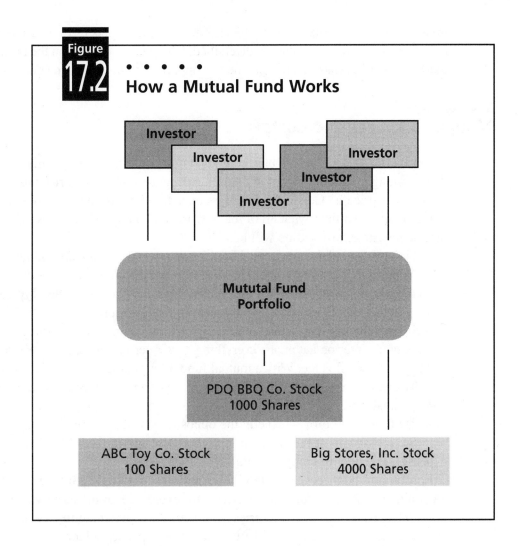

Figure 17.2

• • • • •
How a Mutual Fund Works

Investor

Investor

Investor

Investor

Investor

Mututal Fund Portfolio

PDQ BBQ Co. Stock
1000 Shares

ABC Toy Co. Stock
100 Shares

Big Stores, Inc. Stock
4000 Shares

Important Benefits of Mutual Funds

Mutual funds are an extremely popular way to invest for a number of good reasons. Investing is easy: just send a check or arrange for a transfer of funds from a bank or other account. Whenever you need to get your money out or you decide to make a transfer, simply request a redemption of your shares, and the fund company will process your request quickly. Information is readily available about the fund's holdings, and investment selection and management are done by professionals. Because mutual funds generally hold a number of securities, they are already diversified, which helps to cushion the blow in market downturns and ensures that there is opportunity for growth in good times.

Mutual Fund Fees and Costs

Like anything else we buy, mutual funds come at a cost. Unlike other things, though, mutual funds don't have anything as simple as a price tag to tell us what the price is. Generally, investors have to do a fair amount of detective work to figure out first, what all of the fees are, and then, what the cost of owning the investment over time will be.

First, we'll explain how mutual fund fees work and why understanding them is so important. Let's start, though, with how mutual fund fees are different from the prices associated with other kinds of products and services. Typically when you buy things, price is a pretty clear indicator of product quality. When you choose a luxury car instead of a family sedan, you pay more. And you get more. Leather interior, automatic everything, better performance, better warranty, and higher trade-in value. With a mutual fund, though, higher costs do not necessarily mean more of everything, or even more of anything. Because most ongoing mutual fund fees are deducted from investment returns, higher fees actually translate to lower returns—exactly the opposite of what you're looking for.

So, let's begin at the beginning, with a description of different fees and expenses, and how to compare them.

Mutual fund prices are listed in the newspaper once the fund has reached a certain size. Mutual fund share prices are expressed as net asset values, or NAVs. The NAV is simply the price you would pay per share to buy or sell a mutual fund. The mutual fund listings in the newspaper include current NAV information as of the close of business on the previous day.

Fees are usually expressed as a percentage of the assets in the fund. So, a 4 percent fee represents 4 percent of your money, or $4 in fees for every $100 you invest. Some fees are less than 1 percent, and are expressed in "basis points." A .50 percent fee is one-half of one percent, or $.50 in fees for every $100 of your dollars.

There are really two types of mutual fund fees: sales charges (also called "loads"), and ongoing investment management and operational expenses. No-load and low-load funds, mutual funds that don't charge sales fees or charge very low ones, are becoming increasingly popular, and for good reason. Loads are deducted immediately from the money you invest. They are calculated as a percentage of your total investment, so a 5 percent load on a $100 investment would be $5, for example. Loads are used to pay brokerage firms and brokers themselves for their efforts in selling products. The higher the load percentage, the more of your investment return goes to pay sales commissions. The lower the load, the more your money is invested and working for you.

If the mutual fund listing shows two different NAVs, a "sell" and a "buy," you know you're looking at a fund that carries a sales load. To figure out the size of the load, subtract the sell NAV from the buy NAV, and then divide the remainder by the buy price. This will give you the percentage load being charged by the fund. For example, a mutual fund with a sell NAV of 12.65, and a buy NAV of 12.90 has a load of 1.94 percent (12.90 − 12.65 ÷ by 12.90 × 100).

Another important concept is the idea of "classes of shares." Not all mutual fund shares are created equal, and the mutual fund industry uses different labels to distinguish the different types of shares from one another.

Figure 17.3 shows the three types of loads that are typically imposed and three classes of shares to which they correspond.

There are a number of other expenses associated with mutual funds. Figure 17.4 shows some other expenses you'll find in a prospectus, and what they pay for. In general, operating expenses pay for the actual running of a fund, as opposed to loads and 12b-1 fees, which cover the costs of selling a fund. Together, these fees make up what is called the "expense ratio" of the fund. Some or all of these fees may be charged. The prospectus tells you exactly what you will pay as an investor in a particular fund.

The Lowdown on Loads

Now that you know what all of the fees are, it's equally important to know how they impact your bottom line. It's fairly easy to see the impact of loads— they are simply deducted from money you are investing in a fund. Whenever you pay a load, your investable dollars are reduced by the amount of the load. It is more difficult to see the impact of the other costs, the operating expenses. To understand the impact of operating costs on your investment, turn to the fee table in the front of your mutual fund's prospectus. Scroll down the list of fees until you reach the line for "total operating expenses." This is the percentage

Figure **17.3** • • • • • **Three Types of Loads and Three Types of Shares**	
Type of Load and Type of Share	*How It Works*
Front-end, Class "A"	These range in total cost from 4 percent to 8 percent of your total investment. Front-end loads are deducted from the amount you invest before your money goes into the fund. Using our 5 percent load example above, if you started with $100 you would actually have just $95 to in- vest, after paying a 5 percent front-end load.
Back-end, Class "B"	Back-end loads, as you might guess from their name, are charged when you withdraw money from an investment product. They can be charged as a percentage of an investment, or as a flat fee. These fees are also called "contingent de- ferred sales charges," or CDSCs for short. These fees generally start out in the 5 percent to 6 per- cent range, and drop by 1 percent or so every year over a period of five or six years. By year seven, there is usually no fee imposed when you sell shares of a fund.
Level Load Class "C," or "institutional" shares (may have other letters, too)	Level loads are generally between .25 percent and .75 percent per year on an ongoing basis. These charges are deducted annually from fund assets, just likefront- and back-end loads, and are paid as commissions to brokers and financial advisers. You'll find these charges in the part of the prospectus that talks about the fund's 12b-1 plan and operating expenses. (More information about 12b-1 fees is in Figure 17.4.)

Figure

17.4 • • • • •
Expense Ratio Chart

Type of Operating Expenses	How It Works
12b-1	Usually deducted from a fund's assets (your money!) to pay marketing and related costs. These are a way to cover sales and marketing costs without deducting money from your account balance either up front or when you leave the fund. The portion of the 12b-1 fee that pays commissions is the "level load." Keep in mind that these fees are charged to you every year, while front- and back-end loads are a one-time event. On the plus side, a fund company has an incentive to grow your money, because the higher your account balance, the more they earn in fees.
Exchange Fee	This fee is charged by some fund families when you exchange shares from one fund in a family to another. Exchange fees are generally between $5 and $25.
Account Fee	Usually charged on an annual basis, these fees can range from $10 up to $35 or more for each account you maintain. Often there are account size maximums over which these fees are not charged. This is simply an administrative fee.
Transaction Fees	These fees are assessed as a percentage of assets. They are typically in the 1–2 percent range, and can be assessed on either purchases or redemptions.

of your assets in the fund you will be charged annually, simply to invest in that fund. If you choose a fund that returns 10 percent to you, and the annual expenses are 1 percent, your return is actually just 9 percent. The higher the annual expenses of the fund, the more of your return is eaten up. The impact of loads is a little different. If you invest $10,000 in a fund and it charges a 5 percent front-end load, you'll only invest $9,500. Effectively, the fund needs to earn 5 percent simply to earn back what you paid in fees before you actually start making money. Back-end loads are deducted from the amount of money you redeem from the fund. If you take out $10,000 and the back-end load is 4 percent, you'll take home just $9,600.

Why Pay Mutual Fund Fees?

For the most part, consumers are willing to pay what we see as reasonable fees in return for quality products and services. We think this approach makes a lot of sense, particularly when you are buying investment management services in the form of a mutual fund. You want your fund to pay its managers enough to attract top talent. On the other hand, you need to know what those fees are and feel that they are reasonable. For most investment professionals, a love of making money—for you and for themselves—is why they are in the business.

Be careful, too, not to rush to judgment about buying only no-load funds, or only load funds. The truth of the matter is that there are many load funds that have done an outstanding job for their investors. At the same time, we support paying the most reasonable fees possible, especially where several mutual funds offer similar investment opportunities. Of course, each of us needs to decide how we feel about paying fees, the same way we all find ourselves gravitating to either upscale department stores or their discounting competitors. The hardest part of the fee maze is simply understanding what the fees are and how they impact your bottom line.

The Prospectus

Prospectuses are required by law to disclose pertinent information investors should have before plunking their money into an investment product.

All well and good, but most of them are so long and dry that few investors actually read, let alone digest, what's inside them. This is where you'll find all the details about the fees and expenses on a fund, details about how the fund will invest your money, and usually brief information about the portfolio manager. Prospectuses also include information about the risks of investing in a fund, and housekeeping information, like where to send checks and how to redeem shares. Shorter profile prospectuses offer investors the most critical information included in a prospectus in a much shorter format.

Evaluating Mutual Fund Performance

Mutual fund performance is a funny thing. It is one of the best—one of the only, really—ways to evaluate a mutual fund. At the same time, it's history. We know that history doesn't often repeat itself, although we assume that it will when we buy mutual funds based on historical investment performance.

The best thing to keep in mind when looking at mutual fund performance is a healthy skepticism. Back to our "too-good-to-be-true rule," if it looks outrageously good, it's probably just outrageous. Always keep in mind that there are many ways to present investment performance, and just as many ways to interpret it. Let's start with some of the things you should know when you evaluate investment performance.

Securities regulations require mutual funds to show performance over three time periods: one-year, five-years, and ten-years. Younger funds will show as many years of performance as they have available. Keep in mind that not all time periods are equal—if a period for which returns are reported doesn't include a particularly bad year for that type of investment, that fund will look great compared to its competitors.

Investment performance is typically reported in terms of total return. Total return is all of the growth and earnings your investment in the fund has generated. There are two things that go into measuring total return. First, any dividends or interest an investment has generated, and second, any growth (or loss) in the value of an investment. If you reinvest dividends and capital gains from a fund, your investment returns will include both of these components.

Total returns can be expressed as cumulative returns and as average annual returns. Cumulative returns express how much a fund grows over time. For example, in year one, you invest $10,000 in a mutual fund. Over five years, that fund grows to $14,000. The cumulative return, the difference between 10,000 and $14,000, is 40 percent ($14,000 minus $10,000 equals $4,000 (the growth); then $4,000 divided by 10,000 equals .40, or 40 percent).

Average annual returns express the rate of growth on an annual basis. In our example, the average annual return is 6.96 percent. You may notice that the cumulative return divided by the number of years we're looking at doesn't equal 6.96 percent, our annual return. No, there's no mistake here. Average annual returns include the effect of compounding. So while the rate of growth looks smaller (the actual percentage is smaller), it is being applied to a larger pool of money as your account balance enjoys the effects of compounding.

In our example, in the first year the balance of $10,000 multiplied by the average annual return of 6.96 percent (0.0696) is $696. To begin the second year, add the earned interest of $696 to $10,000 for a total balance of $10,696. Take this starting balance and multiply by 6.96 percent ($10,696 × 0.0696) for a second year interest amount of $744. Add this interest to the balance of $10,696 to begin the third year with $11,440. Keep taking the average annual return and multiplying by the new balance, and then add this amount in until five years of investing is reflected. The total amount at the end of five years will be $13,997.90 (rounded to $14,000 for our example).

Indexes

We talked a bit about indexes in Chapter 8, but let's briefly add a thought or two relative to evaluating mutual fund investment performance. While comparing the returns a fund has delivered to a market index is the best way to see how well a fund manager has done in "adding value" over an unmanaged return, it is not quite an accurate comparison. Why not? Because mutual funds charge fees, and indexes don't. So, even a fund that has very low fees and beats the benchmark may not do so by as wide a margin as you'd like.

Portfolio Managers

Portfolio managers, either individuals or a team, are responsible for the day-to-day management of the fund's portfolio. Look for funds that have managers or teams that have been in place for a while. You want to be sure to hire the people who actually delivered the performance track record that looks so good, not only the person or people who joined up later.

Turnover

Turnover is the rate at which investments are bought and sold. It can apply to individual securities or to mutual fund portfolios as a whole. Turnover is not an indicator of investment performance, but it can have an impact on the amount of capital gains and income dividends a mutual fund portfolio generates for its investors. You should be aware of how growth in a mutual fund portfolio is generated because it can impact the taxes you pay as a mutual fund investor (explained below).

Taxes

Over time, the securities in a mutual fund increase in value. If they are not sold, increases in their value are not taxed. Once a portfolio manager sells appreciated securities, the gains are taxable. These gains are passed to investors, as are losses.

As if things weren't complicated enough, now you have to worry about how investment decisions impact your tax bills. The information in this book is designed to help you make "big picture" investment decisions, not to make recommendations about tax strategies. For that, we recommend you consult your tax adviser. In the meantime, though, there are some things you should know about how taxes impact mutual funds and other investments.

Taxes and Mutual Funds

There are two things to know that will help you understand how mutual funds and taxes interact:

1. For tax purposes, mutual funds are known as "pass through" entities. What does that mean? Simply that mutual funds don't file tax returns, instead, the people who invest in them do.

2. You pay taxes on the growth that your investments experience, whether they are mutual funds, or something else. If your mutual funds are held in a tax-advantaged account, you may defer taxes or avoid them entirely.

Mutual funds pass through both capital gains and income dividends to investors. The value of your investment, everything over the amount you invested originally, is usually a taxable gain.

Taxes and Other Investments

Unless you invest in tax-advantaged investments, you'll owe taxes on the growth your investments experience. Simple, right? Hardly. The tax bill you'll pay has everything to do with the kind of growth your investments enjoy. Is it a capital gain? Is it a short-term or long-term gain? Is it income or a return of invested capital?

Figure 17.5 shows a quick guide to the kinds of taxes due on different types of investment growth.

Figure 17.5 • • • • •
Taxes on Investment Growth

Long-Term Capital Gains	Due on investments held for 18 months or longer. Presently, long-term capital gains rates are lower than income tax rates. Investments held less than 18 months are taxed at a maximum rate of 28 percent.
Short-Term Capital Gains	Due on investments held one year or less. Short-term capital gains rates are the same as ordinary income tax rates.
Income Taxes	Due on income from traditional IRAs and annuities, as well as income and dividends.

Categories of Mutual Funds

Mutual funds are not conveniently labeled by type so that you can pull the flavor you need off mutual fund company product lists. Instead, they are categorized and labeled in a couple of different ways.

Investment objective. Words like capital appreciation, growth and income, growth, etc., define what the fund is trying to accomplish.

Investment style. Investment style talks about the kinds of stocks the investment manager picks. Does she favor a growth strategy, looking for the next Microsoft? Or is hers a value approach, looking for stocks perceived to be "cheap?" If it's a bond fund, does the manager focus on rotating among different sectors of the economy, or does she try to anticipate interest rate changes?

Market capitalization, or market "cap." Stocks are categorized by the size of their market capitalization, or the total value of outstanding stock (stock price multiplied by the number of outstanding stock shares). Small cap stocks are generally companies with $1 billion or less in outstanding stock, large cap stocks are generally companies with $5 billion or more in outstanding stock, and mid-cap stocks (as you would expect) fall somewhere in between large and small cap.

Mutual Fund No-Fee "Supermarkets"

Although they borrow terminology from the grocery business, these have absolutely nothing to do with the way you buy food and household supplies. Mutual fund supermarkets are one of the newest bells and whistles in the mutual fund industry. Offering the ability to invest in mutual funds from many different families, supermarkets provide both consolidated statements and easy telephone or computer switching among mutual funds. What are mutual fund supermarkets? They were traditionally offered by discount brokerage firms and now are offered by some major full-service firms, as well. They typically include hundreds of mutual funds. It certainly seems like this approach makes life easier for investors. But remember the "if it looks to good to be true, it is," rule? Nothing is free in the investment management business, and neither is this new way of buying mutual funds.

There are generally transaction fees charged to investors to participate in the no-fee programs. At the same time, the mutual fund companies available in the supermarkets generally pay a fee to brokerage firms to be included in the programs. Like other fees, this is passed along to investors in the form of increased operating expenses. In addition, these supermarkets don't always provide much in the way of general investment information or education. You're supposed to be paying a lower price for greater convenience, but keep in mind you won't get much else besides your statement and the information on your specific funds. Of course, if you value the ease of switching and receiving fewer pieces of mail enough to pay for these features, mutual fund supermarkets may be a good choice.

This Is Progress?

With the huge increase in the number of mutual funds available to investors (more than 6,800), and the number of people choosing to use mutual funds as their investment vehicle of choice, a new problem has surfaced for many investors. This is the issue of redundancy, of owning several mutual funds that have similar holdings. The consequence of this is that your well-intentioned attempts to diversify your portfolio may actually backfire. You may end up owning three stock mutual funds that all include the same stocks. One fund manager may perceive the company as a growth company, another may feel it is "cheap" and buy it as a value stock. This problem is easily managed by reviewing the actual holdings in each mutual fund you buy. This information is included in annual and semiannual reports that mutual fund companies publish. Information about the top ten or so holdings in a mutual fund's portfolio is generally available by calling the company's toll-free number. After all, if you're going to spend the time becoming an informed investor, and you're going to diversify your investments as a result, it makes sense to spend the time to review your fund holdings and make sure you are as diversified as you think you are. Taking this one step will help to ensure that your investments really are designed to meet the goals you've established for yourself and that there are few "surprises."

Buying Unmanaged Investment Products

There is, of course, more to investing than just mutual funds, although lately it seems hard to believe that, given the huge growth in mutual fund business during the past few decades. You can easily invest directly in stocks, bonds, U.S. Treasury securities, commodities, and any number of more complicated securities.

If you want to buy individual securities and trade them on your own, find either a good online service (see the Resources for Making Investment Decisions section in the back of the book for more information) or a good discount brokerage. Set up a brokerage account and fire away.

A Word about Margin Accounts

Margin accounts offer investors credit to make bigger bets on securities trades in their brokerage accounts. Bigger bets mean, as we all know, bigger wins . . . or bigger losses. Margin accounts are lines of credit offered to investors by the brokerage firms they invest with. Naturally, you will pay interest to the brokerage firm for the privilege of using their money. If you buy securities on margin, the firm will have the right to sell the securities in your account to cover any shortfall that might arise as a result of a change in the value of your securities. Before you experiment with trading securities on margin, remember that credit is "real money": at the end of the day, you owe money to the firm that has given you the credit.

Stocks

Stock picking is an art—and a science. There are as many ways to pick stocks as there are people who pick them. We're not going to go into detail in this book about the process of picking individual stocks—that's a whole other book. We are big fans of the "buy what you know" philosophy when it comes to stock investing. The idea here is to simply pick stocks you know, companies who make products you buy and use. It is equally important to know the details of how a company manages its businesses, and that it's doing a good job making money for itself and its investors. This information is often available directly from the company in the form of annual reports and other materials. You can also check out the library or online resources for company information.

There are two primary styles of stock picking: growth and value. A growth stock philosophy holds with investing in companies that are likely to grow at rapid rates over time. The theory here is that the stock of the company will increase in price, growing your investment very rapidly. The value approach is all about finding bargains, cheap stocks that have taken a beating for one reason or another. Value investors look for companies about to make a turnaround, buy, and look for the stock's price to increase as the company's fortunes do.

A note about initial public offerings, called IPOs. You may learn about companies who are going public, or issuing stock for the first time. This process is called an initial public offering. These can be very exciting for companies, and for investors. If investing in new issues, as these new stocks are called, interests you, learn all you can about the companies you are thinking about investing in. Often stock prices for new issues jump around a lot immediately, and then settle down. Be sure you are comfortable with this level of volatility before you "leap" into a new issue.

Bonds

Bond investing, too, is a discipline unto itself. Because the goal of this book is to help you make investing decisions overall, rather than to help you make individual security selections, we're not going to go into great detail about bond investing here.

It is important to know about one or two important features of bonds we haven't talked about yet. Many bonds offer investors tax benefits. Generally U.S. bonds are exempt from state and local taxes, while bonds issued by state governments are exempt from federal taxes. Here's the formula for figuring out the return that is equivalent to a tax-advantaged return.

Let's assume you invest $10,000 in a bond fund that earns 6 percent, free of federal taxes. Let's assume also that your marginal tax rate (the highest rate at which you pay taxes) is 28 percent. Simply take the interest rate and multiply it by 1 + your marginal tax rate expressed as a percentage ([1 + .28 = 1.28] × 6%). In this case, the number is 7.68. So, you'd need to earn 7.68 percent on your taxable investments just to break even with a tax-advantaged investment. Something to think about, right?

CDs and Treasuries

Certificates of deposit (CDs) are purchased at a bank. Certificates of deposit are essentially an agreement between the depositor (you) and the bank to hold your money for a specified period of time and pay you a stated rate of interest. CDs "lock up" your money for a few months at a time, or even a few years.

Treasuries are securities issued by the U.S. government. While you can buy treasuries through a bank or broker, you can also buy treasury securities directly from the government, eliminating the need to pay a commission. The Treasury Direct program offered through the Federal Reserve bank system allows you to buy, sell, and reinvest directly in treasury securities. Just call your local Federal Reserve Bank or download the forms for the Treasury Direct program from the Bureau of the Public Debt's Web site at www.publicdebt.treas.gov/.

Insurance Products

There are several insurance products that offer an investment component. Annuities, as we discussed earlier, and variable and universal life insurance policies all offer the ability to make investment choices in addition to offering insurance benefits. Some offer choices about the timing of taxes that are due, too. We recommend that once you have taken advantage of all of the tax-advantaged investment accounts available to you, and purchased adequate insurance coverage with single-purpose policies, like term life insurance, then go ahead and take a closer look at insurance products. Again, respect your instincts. Don't buy or invest in anything that doesn't make sense or that you don't fully understand.

Stars Aren't Just in Hollywood

One of the leading firms in the business of evaluating mutual funds is Chicago-based Morningstar. (See the Resources for Making Investment Decisions section in the back of the book for information about how to use Morningstar to make investment decisions.) Morningstar rates mutual funds, assigning a certain number of stars to the funds that offer the best historical risk-adjusted investment returns. The best funds get five stars. In the competitive mutual fund business, how many stars your fund is given is very important. The more five-star funds a mutual fund family offers, the better. Of course, Morningstar's evaluations are not the only criteria to consider.

Opening Investment Accounts

As you begin to make decisions about opening investment accounts, you'll need to make judgments about the kinds of services you're interested in obtaining. Before we provide you with detailed information about different types of professional services and accounts that are available to investors, we'd like to suggest you think first about the different types of services you might be interested in buying.

To simplify the process of deciding what kinds of services you're interested in buying, it's important to decide first what you feel you need in terms of product availability and level of personalized service and information. There are any number of choices, among them:

1. *Consolidated services.* Do you want just one account statement, minimal paperwork, and 24-hour toll-free services?
2. *Cutting-edge services.* Do you want access to technology and software? Education and information?
3. *Local service.* Do you want someone nearby who will get to know you well?
4. *Best of class.* Do you want to pick the best investments from a number of different investment shops?

Take a minute to think about which elements of these categories of service is most important to you. As you read through detailed information about advice and advisers, keep your personal goals and objectives in mind. By taking this approach, you'll be sure to make a decision that makes sense for you, and that you are comfortable with.

Choosing the Right Type of Financial Institution

In order to make sound investing decisions, it's helpful to know a bit about how the investment management business works. It's only fair. After all, the investment industry spends millions every year learning about the behavior of individual investors and how to tailor products to meet their needs. Knowing how the people who are investing money work is part of being empowered to make comfortable choices.

Actually, it's a fairly simple formula. For the most part, investment firms make money charging fees on the money you invest. Because most of the fees are charged on a percentage basis, the more you invest, the more money the firms make. Naturally, these firms have overhead for staff, research, the buildings they occupy, and other business expenses. Many of these expenses stay relatively constant, even as the amount of money the firms have to manage grows. Money management firms grow in two ways: by attracting new investors and by growing the value of the money they are already managing.

There are generally three categories of fees levied by money managers: service fees, asset-based fees, and transaction fees. Service fees are just that, fees charged for specific services. Asset-based fees are based on the total amount of money under management and transaction fees are charged for specific transactions.

Over time, money management can be a very profitable business. Firms can keep costs in line by keeping their staff "lean." Generally, there is a portfolio manager or team responsible for making investment decisions, supported by a research staff or team. Of course, research developed by one team can easily be shared by another group within the same firm, or even sold to other firms. This helps keep costs down and leverages the expenses they incur for investing your money. The amount of assets the firm accumulates grows substantially, but their costs (personnel, overhead, research, etc.) can stay pretty constant.

The good news is that the best money managers help you grow your own nest egg while they earn a living themselves. They are motivated to make money for you because it also directly benefits them. You don't want to assume, however, that anyone is doing the best thing for you. In fact, as they say, knowledge is power, and as a consumer, you deserve to know about, and understand, the products and services you're buying.

Finding Investments and Institutions to Manage Your Money

There are three primary types of financial institutions that invest and manage your money. These are banks, insurance companies, and investment management firms. We'll talk in detail about all three, in terms of what kind of institution is best suited to managing which kind of money, and describing services and fees related to the products they offer. This is not intended to be a comprehensive list of every type of service offered by every bank, insurer, or money manager. That information could fill a book in and of itself. Instead, it is intended as a guide to industry practices. Please check with the financial services firms in your area for detailed information about their products and services. Even firms that may look similar often have differing levels of product offerings and service.

Banks

Banks offer many advantages to consumers, including local presence and local access to your money, the ability to build relationships with bank branch staff, and increasingly, the availability of a broad range of investment products and services, including mutual funds. They also offer insurance on deposits, up to $100,000 per account, per bank. This insurance is provided through the Federal Deposit Insurance Corporation (FDIC). This insurance covers only bank account deposits, including certificates of deposit (CDs), not amounts invested in nonbank investment products, like annuities or mutual funds. In the years since banking deregulation, banks have begun to offer investment and insurance products. Keep in mind though, that many of these products are offered by other companies through the banks; in other words, the banks don't necessarily manufacture the nonbank products, they are just selling them. Sometimes, the products are sold by financial professionals who are essentially manufacturer's representatives, seated in a bank's offices. This is no reflection on the quality of the products. Like everything, they should be evaluated on their own merits.

Because of the traditional "slow to respond" approach that some banks have taken, they can be a bit behind other types of financial institutions in terms of the level of investment education they provide to their customers. There are, of course, some notable exceptions among both the largest banks and smaller, regional institutions. For the most part, though, banks are still in "reactive" mode, rather than "proactive," when it comes to providing broad investment services. The banking industry is trying to play catch-up now, of course, and mergers and acquisitions by banks of providers of other types of financial institutions (mutual fund firms, brokerage houses, etc.) are happening at a frenzied pace. In the future, it's fair to expect that this level of activity will continue and that more investment services will be available from your bank.

In terms of the choices offered, banks have the greatest expertise in the area of banking services, including bank accounts, loans, and credit cards. In general, larger banks offer more in terms of automated services. Smaller banks may offer less automation, but more personal service. Fees can vary widely, too. As a result, assessing which bank is "better" than another can be very difficult. Like everything else in the financial services world, the right bank for you is the bank that offers the features and benefits that make the most sense for you. Our suggestion? Make a list of the banking services and features that mean the most to you, and go talk to the people responsible for customer relations. Ask questions about fees, and go with the bank that seems like the best fit. Remember that banks are competing for your business, so you are in the driver's seat. Be sure to find the best combination of products and services for your needs.

Insurance Companies

Insurance companies generally wear the face of the agents who represent them. In addition to traditional insurance products like life and disability insurance, many insurance agents now represent mutual funds and other investment products available through their own firms or other firms they work with.

There are two fundamental ways to differentiate among insurance products: costs and fees or stability. Because the insurance industry is highly regulated, the costs and fees for some insurance products will be the same no matter who you buy them from. For other products, costs will vary greatly.

The second way to differentiate among insurance companies is by their financial quality and stability. The process of finding out if an insurance company is stable is fairly simple: just ask about their "rating." Insurance companies are rated according to their ability to pay the policy claims that are presented. A company called A.M. Best is the industry leader in terms of evaluating the quality of insurance companies. Standard & Poor's and Moody's also evaluates insurance companies. Your agent should be able to provide you with the most recent Best's or S&P or Moody's report or rating on a company. The A.M. Best's rating book is available at local libraries and indicates company quality on an alphabetical scale, from top, shown as A++ (Superior) to bottom, shown as F (in liquidation). As a general rule of thumb, find an insurance company with an AA or better rating, which indicates excellent or superior ability to pay claims. Ratings take into consideration both qualitative and quantitative analyses of the financial condition of the company. This is an important piece of information. Although not common, there have been cases of insurance companies declaring bankruptcy, so it is important to check up on their financial condition before you purchase insurance. Don't even consider doing business with an insurance company that has not been rated by any of the major firms. And make sure you demand that the agent gives you the information you need to be able to evaluate a company. High pressure sales tactics have been somewhat commonplace in the insurance industry and you need to resist the pressure and, again, feel comfortable with the information you are getting and the company you're doing business with.

As is true of banks, the size of the insurance company is not an indicator of the level of service you will receive as a customer. Be sure to ask your agent about the level of service, information, and responsiveness provided by the company handling your insurance policies. Generally, agents sell products from a variety of companies, and have some options in terms of which companies' products they offer. Increasingly, insurance companies are trying to sell insurance products directly to individuals, by advertising toll-free numbers or sending mailings directly to your home. This approach can help to keep their costs down and, hopefully, this savings is passed along to customers.

Investment Management Firms

This category includes a number of different types of investment management firms. Investors can choose from discount brokerages (Charles Schwab is one of the very biggest and most well recognized), regional brokerage firms (Tucker Anthony in the Boston area, Alex Brown & Sons in New England), firms that position themselves as "boutique" investment managers (Oppenheimer, Neuberger & Berman, etc.), mutual fund companies (Vanguard, Fidelity, and T. Rowe Price are among the largest), and, of course, full-service brokerage firms like Merrill Lynch, Smith Barney, and Paine Webber. This is not a comprehensive list of firms. Individual companies are simply included to give you an idea of the type of company we're describing. The fundamental differences among investment management firms can mean a lot to investors in terms of the specific services and benefits offered to investors, and, of course, the relative costs of the services.

Discount brokerage firms are focused on offering lower-cost services to investors. They offer investors the ability to establish investment accounts, and buy and sell individual securities and mutual funds without benefit of receiving investment advice. Because lower-cost firms tend to offer less in the way of investment advisory services, they can be ideal for more experienced investors who want to make their own decisions and who want to move quickly. To use these firms effectively, you need to know what you want to invest in when you call because they are not likely to offer much help in terms of advising you or directing you to suitable investment choices. They do need to be sure that it is not irresponsible of them to execute the transaction you request, so they are required to obtain background information from you to be certain of the suitability of the transaction.

Regional brokerages tend to be smaller than their national (or global) full-service counterparts. As a result, they can offer more personalized service. They do provide some investment advisory services. They are not generally competing on the basis of price, but on expertise, service, and performance. You can establish an investment account with one of these firms to invest in individual securities or mutual funds. Some of these firms manufacture their own investment products.

The largest national full-service firms have access to lots of resources and a great deal of research information. They usually offer the broadest array of types of accounts and services. Because of the size of their staffs, they can provide you with information about new tax laws, new products, or market changes, among others, very quickly. You can establish an investment account with a national full-service firm. Most have hundreds of local branch offices to invest in individual securities and mutual funds. Many of these firms sell products that they manufacture themselves, their own mutual funds, variable annuities, etc.

Mutual fund companies generally offer and manage their own mutual funds. Increasingly, mutual fund companies (and brokerages) are offering other firms' mutual funds through their "supermarket" approach. Some mutual fund companies have brokerage groups where you can set up an investment account and buy individual securities.

Investment boutiques and investment advisers generally offer specialized investment management products and services, or manage large sums of money for wealthy individual investors. These firms may create individual accounts that are so large they may look like small mutual funds, and they may trade securities for these accounts.

Locating an Investment Management Firm

The best place to start is with a referral. Referrals will generally be to a specific person at an investment firm, rather than to a firm in general. Ask your friends, family, or colleagues where their investment accounts are. But look before you leap. Just because one adviser suits Great Aunt Grace to a T, there is no reason why you should sign on if you don't feel like you're a fit, too. Consult the *Directory of Registered Investment Advisors* at your local library for a complete list of firms. And, of course, don't forget about the phone book. Unfortunately, if you live in a major metropolitan area, the list of firms to contact may be very long. And, if you're seeking an independent investment advisory firm, many of them don't advertise or list their services in the Yellow Pages.

Many full-service firms offer investment seminars on timely investment topics. They are advertised in local papers and can be a good way to get to know both the firms sponsoring the events and the local investment professional that would handle your account. Any firm you select should carry Securities Investors Protection Corporation (SIPC) coverage and should maintain a membership on some major exchange.

History in the community is a good sign. When you visit a local office in your area, check to see if there is an exchange certificate on the wall. Firms are required to post the certificate with the year they were established. Before you sign on with a firm and establish an account, ask for references, preferably from people with profiles similar to yours, and check them out.

Establishing Investment Accounts

You can open different types of accounts at these firms in many different configurations. These accounts can be held individually or jointly, like bank accounts. Accounts can be established with a cash deposit that is then invested in securities. Brokerage firms also offer clients margin accounts, which are essentially extensions of credit to buy securities. The securities in an account are held as collateral against the amount of money you owe the brokerage. Brokerage firms are limited to lending no more than 50 percent of the value of the total securities purchased to individual investors. Margin accounts can only trade in margin stocks, stocks listed on a national exchange, and some other stocks. To establish a margin account you must sign an agreement to arbitration, agreeing not to sue even if something goes wrong with your account. Margin accounts are regulated by the Federal Reserve Bank, the Securities and Exchange Commission, and major national stock exchanges. If you establish a margin account, be sure you understand the regulations and requirements of the account and what they mean to you.

As you can probably guess, the larger the size of an account at a brokerage firm, the more bells and whistles it is likely to have. But because brokerage firms make money on the number of transactions you make, the number of transactions also has an impact on your fees and the level of service you receive. Different levels of service generally relate to both the level of detail in the statements you receive, and the frequency and timeliness of information received for tax reporting. Some accounts also offer check writing features and debit cards. The amounts of money you need to have at a particular firm in order to receive a higher level of service will vary. Generally $5,000 or $10,000 will bump you to a "higher" level account where you would receive more detailed statements, perhaps a tax report nine months into the year and a tax review session in September. Higher account balances may give you increasingly higher levels of service.

Fees

When you buy and sell individual securities in an investment account, you can be charged for a transaction two ways.

First, there can be an agent fee, charged as a straight commission on the transaction. On the transaction confirmation slip you'll find the commission shown in dollars. The second type of fee is a principal fee, included in the total cost of the security. Essentially it's a markup on the price of the investment. The markup must be disclosed to an investor. In general, fees will range from 3 to 5 percent, but the specific fee depends on the complexity of the transaction, and the level of involvement of the person handling it. The question you need to answer for yourself is, do I think this fee is reasonable, given the level of personal involvement of the broker and the nature of the transaction?

If paying transaction fees and commissions doesn't appeal to you, you can join the ranks of investors paying straight investment management fees or wrap account fees. Many firms offer wrap accounts, which include a variety of products and services for a flat fee. These fees are generally in the 1 to 2 percent range. Both of these types of fees are deducted directly from your account balance, so you need to scrutinize your statements to be sure you know when they are deducted and their impact on your investment plan. Keep in mind that, because so many investors are concerned about fees, you may have some leverage if you find your fees objectionable. Talk to the firm you're working with and see if you can get yourself a better deal.

Making the Decision to Hire a Professional Adviser

Just because you are now able to make comfortable and profitable investment decisions for yourself doesn't mean you have to be the day-to-day keeper of your investment books. There are many different types of financial professionals who would love to help manage your money and investments. You may decide that keeping up with the flow of information about your investments is something you'd like to delegate.

The To Delegate or Not to Delegate Financial Tasks Worksheet on the following page will help you decide which functions of managing your financial life you'd like to perform yourself and which ones it might make sense to outsource. We've grouped the tasks by function. Add any tasks that you'd like to the list. This worksheet will be a helpful guide when you begin the process of interviewing people.

To Delegate or Not to Delegate Financial Tasks Worksheet

Task	Pros and Cons of Outsourcing	Pros and Cons of Doing it Yourself	Which Makes More Sense for You (Self or Outsource)?
Keeping current with your accounts			
Keeping current with your individual investments			
"Big picture" planning			
Making asset allocation decisions			
Selecting individual securities			

Buying Investment Advice and Related Services

Like providers of other services, investment advisers come in all shapes and sizes. There are investment professionals out there providing all different kinds of services, using fee structures of their own devising. What we'd like to do here is to give you some information about the range of investment advisory services you are likely to find, and to help you define what you might be looking for. When you've decided what you're looking for, the Resources for Making Investment Decisions section at the back of this book provides you with information about where to go to find individual financial advisers. Whatever you decide, we recommend that you talk to at least three people, in person if you can, and that you check at least three references for each adviser before you make a final decision. How do you really know what you're comfortable with until you have something else to compare to?

There are many investment professionals, and professionals in related fields, who offer financial planning and advice including stockbrokers, insurance agents, fee-based financial planners, trustees, accountants, lawyers, etc. On the one hand, having this much choice about where to buy investment advice is terrific. On the other hand, how do you make a fair comparison? This list, as you can see, includes a number of different kinds of financial professionals, all having different credentialling requirements. The field of financial planning at this point doesn't require standard licensing of practitioners. To help meet the need for increased professionalism among the ranks of advisers, industry groups are now urging financial professions to meet licensing requirements. As a consumer of investment advice, this means the field is wide open. We'll talk about the benefits of working with each type of financial professional, and about what you can expect in terms of fees and services.

Stockbrokers

This group of financial professionals is among the most aggressive in terms of sales approach. While many firms have begun using "softer" sales techniques, some brokerage firms still "cold call" prospects. One of the authors of this book recalls working in a brokerage firm in the late 1980s, where the newest brokers in the firm, housed in cubicles called the "pen" by those lucky enough to have offices, were handed a phone book and expected to find clients by calling folks, day in and day out. Like many professionals, the way stockbrokers are paid can, all too often, be a leading indicator of the way they will service their clients. For the most part, the brokerage business is transaction-based, meaning that brokers get paid when you buy or sell a financial product. Naturally, this means that the focus of their work with you will probably be on buying and selling, rather than holding investments for the long-term. So if you want to open a brokerage account to trade (actively buy and sell) investments, talking to a broker may make a lot of sense.

National, full-service brokerage firms generally have local branch offices. Each branch office has a branch manager. The branch manager can be a good resource to help you find the right person to work with. You can simply call the local office and ask to speak with the branch manager. Then explain your needs, the type of services you are looking for, and the type of person you'd like to work with. The branch manager will be able to point you in the direction of the broker most likely to fit the bill. If you prefer, ask for an appointment with the branch manager. This will give you an opportunity to see the office and get a feel for how it operates, without having made a commitment to a specific broker.

To help new recruits get a head start, some brokerage firms give rookies the opportunity to be broker-of-the day. The honor, of course, is rotated among investment professionals who are still in business-building mode. Most established brokers don't participate. For the broker-of-the-day, this means that any walk-ins or phone-ins that come to that office that day are directed to him or her. As a result, you could find your simple call asking for information about a brokerage firm directed to a newly minted investment professional. Who knows, you might luck out and find someone wonderful that way. On the other hand, don't hesitate to ask some hard questions.

To establish a brokerage account, you'll need to complete some paperwork about your financial situation. Be as complete as possible in your answers, and if the questionnaire leaves out something that is important to you, be sure to tell your broker what's on your mind. This process is the best way for the broker to help you make transactions that are right for you and your financial situation. You can open up a brokerage account with as little as a few hundred dollars. The only consequence to being a "small" investor is that you're unlikely to get a lot of attention from your broker. One note to point out, minors cannot open brokerage accounts by themselves.

The commissions you will pay your broker are set by the investments themselves, and can range from zero on a money market fund to a high of 7 percent or so on limited partnerships and other, more complex, investment products. The fees charged for trading individual securities are set by the firms themselves. Because brokers get paid for transactions, the more business you generate for your broker, the more attention you're likely to get. Always, always, ask your broker how she or he is getting paid on transactions executed for you. Keep in mind that brokers don't get paid for providing customer service, advice, or for hand holding. Many brokers, recognizing that investors want advice and education, are beginning to offer that to their clients in the form of seminars. Unless their firm provides a way for them to get paid for this type of service, remember that they are doing it to attract transaction business.

Brokers can have a number of different credentials. They are always Registered Representatives, registered through their firms with the National Association of Securities Dealers (NASD). If they sell stocks and bonds, they must hold a Series 7 license. If they sell other financial products, like life insurance, they must also have special licenses to do so. They may hold additional credentials, like Certified Financial Planner (CFP) or Chartered Financial Consultant (ChFC). Some may also hold the Uniform Investment Advisor registration, but because brokers don't get paid to advise, not many do. In order to obtain the Series 7 license and other securities registrations, brokers have to study for—and pass—exams administered by the NASD. They also must continue their education or the NASD can pull their licenses.

Once you have established a brokerage account, you will begin receiving statements. Read them. Carefully. Watch for any transactions you did not authorize, or more activity than you actually initiated. Be sure that the investments in your account (the statement should list the current market values for your holdings) make sense to you. If you don't like what you see, or don't understand what you see, ask your broker. Don't feel uncomfortable if the statements are hard to understand; they are notoriously difficult to decipher and understand. Be sure to ask for a translation of any abbreviations and symbols. (The authors sympathize; after many years in the investment business, we still don't look forward to interpreting account statements.)

Here's a start on the list of questions to ask of and about your broker before signing on. Add your own, too.

- How many clients do you work with?
- How long have you been selling stocks and bonds?
- Where did you receive your training?
- What did you do before you became a broker?
- What credentials do you hold?
- Do you have a specialized area of knowledge?
- How do you get paid? Ask this question for each transaction you initiate.
- Does your broker have a record of disciplinary action? Call the National Association of Securities Dealers toll-free hot line at 1-800-289-9999 to find out.

A word about private accounts. Some brokerage firms offer the option of private account management for their largest investors. This means that a large chunk of money will be managed by a single investment manager, usually an investment pro who manages a mutual fund or an account for a business or pension fund (an institutional investor). This type of service is not something that most investors will use, but as your assets increase over time, your accounts may well command this level of service.

Investment Advisers

The category of financial professionals who call themselves financial advisers includes people with many different types of credentials and backgrounds, providing many different kinds of investment related services. In fact, many stockbrokers describe themselves as financial advisers.

To simplify, we've broken financial advisers into three different categories:

1. Financial planners, who provide all-around financial planning services
2. Independent investment advisers, who actively manage your portfolio
3. Independent investment advisers, who provide specific investment advice for a fee

Financial Planners

Financial planners take the most comprehensive view of your financial situation, generally looking at your entire financial picture and helping you with solutions to many different financial issues in the context of your overall needs. Financial planners are generally paid a set fee for their services, or an hourly rate for their time. Some charge fees based on the total assets (amount of money) they are advising you about. Financial planners should be very focused on providing you with information you need to make your own comfortable and profitable investment decisions. Often financial planners will help with tax planning, although it always makes sense to get tax advice from a tax professional, especially if your tax picture is at all complicated. Some financial planners will go beyond just planning, and actually sell you investment products. Others, called fee-only planners, do not get paid commissions for the sale of individual securities. If you're not sure how a planner gets paid for services or for selling securities, ask.

Typically, planners will provide a complimentary first meeting, to assess your needs and to give you an opportunity to assess them. The output from the planning process is usually a document prescribing specific changes to be made to your financial picture. Look for planners who will include in your plan specific recommendations about the types of investments that make sense for you. While general guidelines are a good first step in the financial planning process, be sure that your planner provides you with enough specifics to allow you to move forward and actually buy products that will make the plan a reality. If you don't see what you need, ask for it. Many planners assume you will probably invest in mutual funds, along with many other shareholders, rather than selecting individual stocks and bonds on your own.

Many professional financial planners hold the Certified Financial Planner designation. The CFP is a professional credential indicating that the planner has met the qualifications set by the Certified Financial Planner Board of Standards, Denver, Colorado. To receive this designation, a professional must understand a cross section of subjects including investment analysis, taxes, employee benefits, and insurance and estate planning. The person must then pass a 10-hour exam covering all of these topics, and more. A financial planner may also hold other securities licenses and designations such as: Certified Public Accountant (CPA), which requires the person to pass a comprehensive exam in taxes and accounting; Chartered Financial Consultant (ChFC), which requires the person to pass a financial services curriculum, with an emphasis on life insurance; Chartered Life Underwriter (CLU), which requires the person to be trained in life insurance; and Personal Financial Specialist, which is given to accountants who include 750 hours of financial planning, over three years, in their practice and who pass an exam which covers topics like retirement planning. Each designation requires the person holding it to take continuing education courses.

Without regard to the designation a planner might hold, the following list of questions is important to cover with anyone you are considering to use for financial planning. The questions are similar to those you would need to ask a stockbroker. Again, add your own specific questions to the list.

- What specific services do you provide and what are the fees for these services?
- How many clients do you work with?
- How long have you been providing financial planning advice?
- Where did you receive your training?
- What did you do before you became a planner?
- What credentials do you hold?
- Do you have a specialized area of knowledge?

Investment Advisers

There are two categories of investment advisers, as we mentioned above. Investment advisers can either manage portfolios themselves, or they can direct you to specific investments. The difference between financial planners and advisers is typically the scope of the services provided. Investment advisers will only look specifically at a client's investments, while planners generally look at your complete financial picture. The distinction is similar to that of seeing two different kinds of doctors, a general practitioner and a specialist. Investment advisers need only register with the Securities and Exchange Commission, the primary governing body for the securities business, and with the state in which they are doing business. Some states are now requiring advisers to register with the NASD as well. The adviser must file an ADV form, which is their application to become an investment adviser. This ADV form is something you should ask to see, and includes background information on the principals of a firm, including educational information and birth dates, among other tidbits. In fact, if you're at all hesitant to ask questions about your adviser's background, such as where he or she went to school, you can simply read this information on the ADV form.

Finding investment advisers can be a more involved process than finding stockbrokers or financial planners. There is, unfortunately, no central resource for advisers that is easily accessible to consumers, although, of course, many are listed in the Yellow Pages. The best bet is to ask people you know who they use for financial advice. Whether you find someone through a referral or through the Yellow Pages, ask to talk to a couple of clients whose profiles are similar to yours. Again we say: always, always check the references.

The fee structure for investment advisers is a little different from the way brokers and planners charge, too. Most charge a percentage of the assets they manage, and the percentage goes down as the size of the assets goes up. A typical fee schedule might look like 1 percent of the first $500,000 under management, 0.75 percent of the next $500,000, and so forth. The more money you invest, the lower the percentage figure you will be charged on your total assets. Fees are typically billed quarterly and often deducted directly from the investment account. If you have $100,000 to $200,000 to invest, you can hire an investment adviser to create a customized portfolio for you, buying stocks and bonds for your individual account. If you have less than that, you probably want to hire an adviser who will direct you toward mutual funds. Because investment advisers are not generally also brokers, there are additional transaction costs that will be incurred when securities are traded for your account.

Expect an investment adviser to spend a fair amount of time getting to know you, and be sure to take the time to get to know her, too. It is in everyone's best interest to be sure that your objectives fit with the expertise of the adviser. Take all the time you need—before you sign an advisory agreement—to feel comfortable with the relationship.

Because the adviser will ask you some pointed questions, too, be sure to think through how the pool of money you're interested in having them manage fits with your overall financial picture. They should also ask you what your short- and long-term expectations are for this money. Be prepared to spend a lot of time on the topic of investment risk and your feelings about risk-taking. Alarm bells should go off for you if the conversation doesn't include these topics. If you don't talk about these important issues, the adviser won't have the information needed to manage your money in a way that will help you meet your investment goals.

What kinds of questions should you ask when you sit down with a potential investment adviser? Don't be afraid to ask if there is any legal action pending against the adviser. Yes, this is a very direct question, but if the record is clear, he or she has nothing to hide. If there is something going on, that should raise a red flag, too. Ask about background and level of experience, too. Some specific questions to ask include the list below, but as always, don't be afraid to add your own questions. A responsible investment adviser will help you with questions you should ask them, and will probably give you more information than you asked for. An adviser who won't take the time to get to know you, or won't give you references to talk to, is not someone with whom you want to entrust your financial future.

- What is your investment approach?
- What kinds of stocks do you focus on?
- How do you deal with investment risk?
- What is your approach to asset allocation? Specifically, how much of the portfolio is in stocks, in bonds, and in cash?
- How quickly will you investment my money? (The "right" answer here is over a reasonable period of time, several months at least. The goal is to take advantage of the principles behind dollar cost averaging and to "average" you into the market.)
- What investment performance have you delivered to your clients, relative to your clients' goals?

For advisers managing investment portfolios, you will want to set clear performance expectations. Performance expectations are goals, really, a way to analyze their investment performance based on what you need to achieve. How often should you review investment performance? While performance will probably be reported to you on a quarterly basis, you will benefit from taking a longer-term view. Of course, if something unexpected occurs, don't hesitate to make a move. But be careful not to overreact. If you have any questions about what's happening with your money, ask. At the same time, be clear with your adviser about how involved you'd like to be, and nail down good answers to any and all concerns before you get started. This relationship needs to get off on the right foot, with a high level of trust, in order to be successful.

There are several agreements you will need to sign as your investment account is opened. The first is an advisory agreement, giving your adviser the ability to make investment decisions for you. (It's easy to see why knowing the person well is so important, isn't it?) The second will be with a brokerage firm or bank, which is the place where your account will actually exist. Don't give an adviser permission to withdraw money from your account for anything other than fees, and never give ownership or possession of your money to anyone else. Take the time to read any agreement you sign.

A Word about Insurance Agents and Other Financial Professionals

Many financial professionals, accountants, and insurance agents in particular, are often called upon by clients to offer financial advice. Unless these professionals are qualified, credentialled, and licensed to do so, they should not be providing financial advice simply because they are in a related field. Look for the designations of Chartered Financial Consultant (ChFC), Chartered Financial Analyst (CFA), or Certified Financial Planner (CFP), and be sure to ask all of the pertinent questions you can think of.

Trustee Services

Trustee services, provided by banks and professional private trustees, include a broad range of investment advisory and financial services. The services provided by trustees can include help with income tax returns, paying bills, counseling you on how much money you need to live on, helping you with major purchases like houses and cars and may even include bringing in an investment adviser to ensure you get the best advice available. Some of these services may be provided by the trustee themselves, or the trustee will bring these other services to you.

Trustee services are available to people who have, in general, a minimum of $100,000 to invest. Depending on where you live and the size of the institution offering the trustee services, this minimum can be much higher. What kind of investor are trustee services right for?

- People who have never had much money but are starting to earn large incomes. If you're earning more than $100,000 a year and have no time—or no inclination—to get involved in the process of managing your own assets, tax planning, or other tasks related to investing, trustee services may make a lot of sense. Perhaps you have company stock options and need to explore diversifying your portfolio. While your assets may not be substantial today, they may indeed grow to be.
- People who, through divorce or losing a spouse, are alone and newly in charge of making financial decisions, perhaps reluctantly so. These investors often don't know where to begin—and they know that they don't know—and want advice and counsel.
- People who have inherited wealth and will be dealing with complex tax and estate issues.
- People who have received a large lump-sum retirement plan distribution.
- Someone who has won an award in a personal injury lawsuit and needs to invest carefully in order to live on these assets.

The fees for trustee services are charged as a percentage of assets. The fees generally start between 1 and 1½ percent and decrease as the assets under management increase. If you like the sound of trustee services, but don't meet the account size minimums, you may be able to make an arrangement to invest through a broker, and separately pay a trustee an hourly fee for services. Like all other financial professionals, a trustee should explain his or her fee to you, and should be very clear about what the fee encompasses in terms of the services you'll receive. Unlike other financial professionals, trustees will actually have all of the rights (the ability to make all of the decisions) to trust property, except the right to its benefit. The right to benefit from the assets, is, of course, reserved for the beneficiary, you. Trustees are responsible for managing the money for your sole interest, not theirs.

How do you find a trustee? If you are comfortable with your bank, ask if they have a trust department. If not, check out some of the larger banks in your area. There may also be a bank that specializes in trustee services in your area. Talk to them, too. Ask your attorney or accountant for a referral. Many attorneys have relationships with bank trust departments and can refer you to someone they know personally. In some areas, Boston most of all, many lawyers and law firms act as private trustees themselves.

How Do You Buy Other Professional Services?

Buying investment advice, for many of us, is a very different process from buying other kinds of professional services and advice. For some reason, the criteria for buying financial advice and related professional advice are often different than the criteria for selecting providers of other kinds of services. It has been our experience, from talking to many individuals who buy these services, and from talking to providers of the services themselves, that the problem lies with how comfortable people are asking tough questions of the people providing investment advice and information. For the most part, people push back harder, ask more pointed questions, demand more references, etc., of other service people than they do of investment advisers. This hesitancy seems related to how competent people feel themselves to be in evaluating investment professionals.

This is unfortunate, for both the buyers and the sellers of investment advice and services. Let's look at a similar kind of process, selecting a doctor for ourselves or for our child. Most of us have not gone to medical school, so while we look at the medical school diplomas on the wall in the doctor's office, unless the doctor attended a brand-name school, we don't have a lot to go on. So we choose our doctors based on criteria we feel we are qualified to apply. Does the doctor have a pleasant personality? Is the office friendly and accommodating of emergency visits? Are questions answered thoroughly and carefully? Are the diagnoses correct? Are the referrals to other doctors we also like? Why should you approach choosing a professional investment adviser or service provider any differently?

In order to find a common ground with a professional investment adviser, it is very helpful to have a way to evaluate them. This exercise will give you a tool for evaluating a professional investment adviser or service provider.

Step One: Create a list of characteristics that are important to you in an investment professional.

This list should include both specific services you would like to have available as well as more subjective criteria, like how well your questions are answered?

Here's an example of what a list of important characteristics might look like.

1. Provides plenty of information
2. Takes the time to explain concepts I'm not familiar with
3. Doesn't push me to make decisions I'm uncomfortable with
4. Fees are reasonable
5. Provides financial planning services for my overall financial picture

Step Two: Use your list as a way to evaluate the investment professionals you are choosing from.

Fill in the list of important characteristics and the names of the providers you are talking to, and fire away. The questions on your list either should be answered during a general presentation, or in response to a specific question from you. Filled in, this grid will give you a good idea of where these professionals stand in relation to one another, and in terms of your objective criteria for evaluating them. Remember, please, that your "gut" is as good a tool as any objective criteria. When police officers—or moms—make decisions based on a "feeling," it's validated as an "instinct," based on experience. How does this apply to selecting an investment professional? If it doesn't feel right to you, it probably isn't right, and you should probably continue making calls or meeting with people until you find someone who feels right, is qualified to help you, and who offers the services you need.

Evaluating Prospective Advisers Worksheet

Important Characteristics	Provider 1:	Provider 2:	Provider 3:
1			
2			
3			
4			
5			
6			
7			
8			
9			
10			

Okay, so now you've got the information you need to begin to make your own decisions about where to begin investing, or where to make changes in your current situation. If you're thinking to yourself, "there's a lot to do and a lot of information I need to know and have," you're right. Sifting through the information and finding the "stuff" that's most important is, we believe, the biggest challenge individual investors face today. We were reminded, as we compiled information, just how much is out there—and how confusing it can all be.

(continued)

So, what are you going to do? Let's recap the process you've been exposed to as you've worked through the information and exercises in this book.

1. Develop a well thought out, personalized financial plan including goal setting, time frames, and prioritization. Most importantly, take the time to really "see" your goals—use visual reminders.

2. Think through the unavoidable, but somewhat manageable, risk aspect of investing and determine your personal comfort zone for risk. Consider the goals you've set, the investment choices to meet those goals and the underlying risks inherent in each investment choice.

3. Become acquainted with different products, people, and financial institutions that stand ready to serve your investing needs.

4. Make a list of the things that are most important to you and the "must have's" as you go through your investing process.

5. Take that list and focus on the people, or services that are most likely to fit your personal needs—you can immediately eliminate many of the options out there just because they don't fit the broad categories that are important to you.

6. Begin a search for the type of people, products, and services that you think will meet your needs.

7. Determine whether you want to become a knowledgeable investor who is self-reliant and makes your own decisions and choices, or an investor who is knowledgeable but prefers to depend on someone else for advice and direction on what to do.

8. Get information you need about options you think might be right for you. Ask questions—until you really understand the answers—and begin to narrow down your choices.

9. Look at your existing investment portfolio and the choices you've made to determine where you will begin anew and where you will make changes to existing investment allocations.

10. Choose the people, products, and institutions that best fit your needs and begin to implement your new strategy and investment choices. Never work with anyone who makes you feel uncomfortable or who won't answer all your questions.

11. Most of all, don't rush. Investing for wealthbuilding is a long-term process and the best thing you can do is to take the time to make the right decisions for you. Don't worry about missing the great market uptick that may happen this week or next. A focus on wealthbuilding, over time, will give you the financial resources you need to meet your most important goals.

12. Trust yourself and your instincts. Remember, it is your money, your goals, your wealth, and your financial security that you're dealing with. No one but you and your loved ones should tell you what is best for your financial wellbeing.

Step Three: If any of these twelve steps don't sound familiar or if you skipped one, review that section of the book.
     We've outlined a logical progression which flows the way the investment decision-making process should flow. Perhaps, as you've read through the material you fear repeating financial mistakes from the past. Don't panic; use this new information to chart a different path from now on. Not many decisions are *completely* irreversible—so, take a clean sheet of paper and start over. By thoughtfully taking the time to go through each step, including filling in the tables and gathering your personal information, it will lead to easier decisions about what to do next.

• • • • •

Building wealth does not happen overnight. It's a process which requires conscious thinking about what information you have, and what you need to obtain, defining specifically what goals—in priority order—are most important to you, looking critically at your current financial situation and taking steps to save money and invest wisely to meet future goals. As difficult as life can be, and as expensive as it can be, there are ordinary people every day who are accumulating wealth and meeting their financial goals. By taking the time to read through this book and—most importantly—act on the information contained in it, you too can be on the road to building wealth and making profitable and comfortable investment decisions. We wish you the best!

Resources for Making Investment Decisions

This resource section is designed to give you some concrete "next steps" to take as you continue to gain knowledge about investment decision making. We found some interesting things as we gathered information to put this section together. We found that there is much more information out there than any one person can reasonably digest. And we found that many sources of information were like icebergs—you could start at the tip, sure, but as you explored, there was so much more information you could hardly hope to get your arms around it all.

A complete listing of all available sources of information about investing out there could fill a book itself. The actual information could, and does, fill libraries. To help you, we've evaluated many of the sources of information available to individual investors and categorized them according to how they can help you with investment decision making. These sources will, we hope, provide you with actionable information—and also lead you to more sources of actionable information in your quest to become a knowledgeable investment decision maker.

Finding Advice and Investment Advisers

If you want to take the information from this book, now that you've done your goal setting and you understand more about your risk tolerance, and contact an investment professional to help you further, the following organizations can help you locate a financial adviser. The financial adviser you select should be one with whom you feel comfortable. Be sure to interview at least three people, and always check references before you make a decision to work with anyone. This is your money, and your time, so don't be afraid to ask any questions that you may have. If the planner won't take the time to talk with you and answer all of your questions, move on to the next name.

There are primarily three ways that financial advisers get paid for working with you. An adviser should *always* disclose to you how you will be paying him or her. You should always ask, too! First, they can be fee-based planners, which means they charge a flat hourly fee to work with you strictly to develop a plan. A good planner will help you with needs analysis and goal setting and will probably also create an implementation strategy for you. The planner will tell you what kinds of funds or investments you should look for but won't find the investments for you or invest the money on your behalf. Any planner should be willing to spend time with you in a first consultative meeting at no charge.

The second way a financial adviser can get paid is by receiving a commission or fee from the investments you select. This means the adviser is getting paid directly from the investments they are directing you to invest in. A good adviser will suggest only investments that are right for you, as opposed to those that yield the adviser the best compensation.

The third possible compensation structure is a combination of fee-based and commissioned.

There are many types of planners and advisers. First let's look at the different kinds of credentials one can hold, and next we'll list the organizations to contact to find someone who is right for you.

Certified Financial Planner. This is the credential that holds practitioners to the most rigorous standards. A Certified Financial Planner (CFP) has received the designation after passing a ten-hour examination administered by the Certified Financial Planner Board of Standards, Denver, Colorado. Areas of knowledge that are tested include: investment analysis, taxes, insurance, estate planning, and employee benefits. In addition to passing the exam, a CFP must have three years of work experience in the field and participate in ongoing education courses related to the field.

Chartered Financial Analyst (CFA). Professionals with this designation adhere to a rigid set of guidelines based on SEC standards and rules. The CFA designation is awarded by the Association of Investment Management and Research (AIMR) to people who pass a series of three comprehensive exams and who have at least three years of investment experience.

Chartered Financial Consultant (ChFC). This designation is awarded to someone who has studied financial services with an emphasis on life insurance. In addition to passing the financial services curriculum, a ChFC must have three years of work experience in the field and participate in ongoing education courses related to the field.

Certified Public Accountant (CPA). CPAs have passed a rigorous exam which focuses on taxes and accounting. CPAs must be licensed in the state, or states, where they practice. CPAs who carry the designation of Personal Financial Specialist (PFS) include 750 hours of financial planning in their practices over three years and pass an exam on topics such as financial planning and retirement planning. Ongoing education courses in related subjects are required.

The National Association of Personal Financial Advisers (NAPFA). 355 West Dundee Road, Suite 107, Buffalo Grove, IL 60089; toll-free number: 888-FEE-ONLY (333-6659) for inquiries. NAPFA, established in 1983, is a nonprofit organization that advances the practice of fee-only financial planning. A financial planner belonging to NAPFA must have three years' experience in comprehensive fee-only planning, have a college degree or its equivalent, have formal financial planning training, be in compliance with registration laws, and submit a financial plan for approval. The planner may *not* receive any economic benefit when a client implements the planner's recommendation including any commissions, rebates, awards, finder's fees, and bonuses.

NAPFA provides a nice questionnaire that you can use to interview a prospective financial adviser to be sure you are covering all of the important questions.

The Institute of Certified Financial Planners (ICFP). 3801 E. Florida Avenue, Suite 708, Denver, CO 80210; toll-free number: 800-282-PLAN (7526).

The ICFP is the nation's largest professional financial planning association of Certified Financial Planners (CFP) practitioners who have completed educational and professional requirements, and adhere to a professional code of ethics. In your preliminary discussions with a CFP professional you should request and receive a disclosure document that details that person's experience, education, compensation, services offered, and potential or real conflicts of interest.

When you call the ICFP and give them your zip code, they will provide you, free of charge, a directory and biographical profile of up to three CFP licensees in your area. You can receive this information either over the telephone or via mail.

The ICFP provides a nice brochure with twelve questions to be considered in selecting a qualified financial planning professional. It aptly states in the brochure that "Choosing a financial planner is as important as choosing a doctor or lawyer."

The International Association for Financial Planning (IAFP). 5775 Glenridge Drive NE, Suite B-300, Atlanta, GA 30328-5364; toll-free number: 888-806-PLAN (7526); Web site: www.iafp.org. The IAFP, founded in 1969, is the oldest and largest nonprofit organization of its type in the world. IAFP states that they bring together individuals and companies committed to using the financial planning process to help people achieve their financial goals.

The IAFP has as its members both financial planners serving individuals and corporations, and companies serving financial planners by providing financial products and services.

When you call the IAFP you will receive, within five to ten business days, detailed backgrounds and information about five advisers in your geographic area that match the criteria you have specified. The background includes information about the adviser's experience, services offered, educational background, licenses and designations held, and an overview of the adviser's practice. This referral program can also be accessed through the IAFP's web site listed above.

In addition, IAFP provides consumers with two free brochures explaining the financial planning process and how to select a financial planner and an interview guide sheet to help in the fact-gathering and selection process. They also have available, free of charge, a brochure on funding a college education.

If you want more information on finding advice but you don't want to deal with an investment adviser, there is an option available for individuals who want to become effective independent managers of their own investments.

The group also has a publication called "Computerized Investing (CI)" that reports the latest developments in software products and online services for investors. Subscriptions to CI are $30 a year for members and $40 a year for nonmembers.

Finding, Comparing, and Evaluating Investments

If you feel that you have a good handle on your financial goals and your financial plan, you may want to seek out investments on your own to complete your portfolio. In order to make the process of finding investments, comparing those investments to others, and evaluating which investments are right for you, there are many resources available. The primary sources of information come in the form of newsletters, Web sites, magazines, and books. We've located some of each, so you can select your preferred method of learning.

Newsletters*

Select Information Exchange (SIE). Toll-free number: 800-743-9346. SIE provides a trial plan for selecting an investment newsletter service by allowing you to sample several different newsletters before you decide which ones are best suited to meet your needs. Their catalog tells you the subscription rate for each newsletter.

For $69 SIE provides you with your choice of four investment newsletters, each for a five-month period. You receive a catalog detailing information on 165 diverse publications.

SIE also offers a special for $11.95 where you choose 20 titles chosen from more than 140 publications for one to five trial issues.

SIE has done a lot of the work for you by selecting 165 titles of the best performing, most popular newsletters from nearly 500 that SIE represents. If you are interested in newsletters as a source of information, we strongly recommend you pay the less than $12 fee to receive samples of 20 newsletters. This way you can see what you are getting and know, before you subscribe, that the information is right for your needs.

---

*While prices are listed for each of these newsletters, most are available, free of charge, at your local library.

Morningstar. 225 West Wacker Drive, Chicago IL, 60606; 312-696-6000; Web site: www.morningstar.net. Morningstar provides several excellent tools for investors who want to make their own decisions and need access to information about specific investments and how they compare to other investments.

In the category of print products, Morningstar has the following options available:

1. Morningstar Mutual Funds—this resource includes detailed, full-page reports on 1,650 open- and closed-end funds, as well as editorial commentary about the industry, trends, and individual funds. Published bi-weekly, the annual subscription rate is $425. A three-month trial is available for $55.

2. Morningstar No-Load Funds—this resource provides detailed, full-page reports on nearly 700 no-load and low-load funds. It includes similar information as listed above but is geared to investors interested primarily in no-load funds. You receive issues every four weeks for the one-year rate of $175. A $45, three-month trial is also available.

3. Morningstar Mutual Fund 500—this softbound book contains a year-end synopsis of the best performing funds in the industry. The one-page reports give you the year-end information on the fund's performance, Morningstar rating, analysis, portfolio holdings, and fundamental analysis statistics. The cost is $35.

4. Morningstar Variable Annuity/Life Performance Report—this monthly reference guide offers information on more than 5,800 individual sub-accounts, 300 variable annuity policies, and 120 variable life policies. It contains ranking on the leaders and followers in each of Morningstar's categories, category ratings, and performance and fee information. A one-year subscription costs $295 for monthly, $145 for quarterly, and $45 for a current issue.

5. *Morningstar Investor,* published monthly, for an annual rate of $79, this newsletter contains research and commentary on investment issues of the day. There are monthly features such as "Planner's Corner" that offer advice on portfolio management through guest certified financial planners. It also contains statistics on 500 funds hand-picked by Morningstar's analysts.

Value Line. 220 East 42nd Street, New York, NY 10017-5891; 212-907-1500. Value Line provides a number of resources for investors interested in doing research on their own and making their own stock selections. In addition to the newsletters listed here, Value Line offers a line of electronic publications and a line of mutual fund investments.

The Value Line Investment Survey contains investment recommendations updated and issued weekly for an annual subscription cost of $570. The survey covers 1,700 equity issues and gives more than just descriptive information. For each stock in its universe it offers year-ahead and three- to five-year probable, relative price performance, projections of key financial measures, and concise, objective commentary on current operations and future prospects. It offers one-stop "shopping" for people seeking investment information on specific stocks.

The Value Line Mutual Fund Survey, annual subscription of $295, provides full-page profiles of 1,500 leading mutual funds. Annual subscribers receive condensed coverage of an additional 500 newer funds plus unique profiles and analyses on 99 of the nation's leading fund families.

The Value Line No-Load Fund Advisor, annual subscription of $107, is geared to investors who want to select only no-load and low-load mutual funds for their portfolio. In addition to all the information you need on 600 leading no- and low-load funds, each issue features strategies for maximizing total return with special attention given to tax considerations.

Value Line also offers surveys covering emerging companies, options, and convertibles.

Newspapers

The Wall Street Journal. 800-JOURNAL (568-7625); Web site: www.info.wsj.com. This daily publication is hands-down the required reading by any serious investor who wants to be well-read and up-to-date on what's happening in business and industry. Dow Jones & Company, publishers of the *Journal* also publish a number of other useful newspapers such as the *National Business Employment Weekly.* They have an Educational Service Bureau to provide professors and students with case studies from the *Wall Street Journal.* The online version is a great way to keep up to date and save paper. The annual subscription rate is $175.

Web Sites

www.kiplinger.com. Kiplinger's is a leading provider of personal finance and business forecasting guidance in the United States. They offer information in many different formats, including business letters, magazines, books, software, video- and audiotapes, and more. Lots of good information is available on their comprehensive Web site, including the ability to subscribe to *Kiplinger's Personal Finance Magazine,* an excellent source of information.

www.mfmag.com. This Web site allows you to hotlink directly to the Internet site of dozens of fund families, fund brokers, fund publications, and other fund organizations. A charter membership costs $9.99 per month (charged to your credit card) and gives you unlimited access to this information plus fund profiles, charts and data on more than 7,000 funds, fund screening, dozens of variables on those 7,000 funds, fund closing quotes, top-performing funds of the day, and performance rankings.

In addition, as a member of Mutual Funds Online you can get discounts on several well-known magazines such as *Fortune, Money,* and *Worth.* You also receive charter subscriber discounts on twelve different investment advisory services such as *Fidelity Forecaster, Mutual Fund Weekly,* and *Fund Watch.*

www.thomsoninvest.com. This site charges a membership fee of $9.95 a month, or $89.95 a year, and includes a live ticker for real-time quotes, the ability to create a personalized portfolio, access to new information, and extensive research tools. Registering as a guest with the site, which is free, gives people the ability to access news and create personalized portfolios.

Magazines

Money. 800-633-9970 (for orders and customer service). Whether you are the kind of person who likes to read magazines so you can flip to specific articles of interest or if you take the cover-to-cover approach, you may find *Money* magazine helpful as a step toward becoming a knowledgeable investor. This monthly publication does an excellent job of giving both general information and specific help on saving and investing. It covers a broad range of topics from funding a college education to where to get the best mortgage rate.

Money is very easy to read and understand and it provides a wealth of information on where to get additional information!

Smart Money. The Wall Street Journal Magazine of Personal Business, 800-444-4204 (orders). This monthly magazine offers a great deal of information for investors on all kinds of issues involving saving and investing. It does an excellent job of providing consumers with a great deal of useful information on not only specific investments, such as mutual funds, but also the best deal on, for example, a cellular phone. Its format is a little harder to read for the less serious investment reader, but the information is definitely worth getting.

Books and Other Print Materials

There are so many books available to "help" you save and invest your money wisely that it would take a separate resource to list all of them. Some of the books that are available are easy to understand, others require that you receive an advanced degree in investing. We have selected a few specific recommendations for you based on what topic you are interested in.

Internet investing. If you're interested in learning more about investing and doing it over the Internet, pick up *Expert Investing on the Net,* by Paul B. Farrell, J.D., Ph.D., published by John Wiley & Sons. This book gives excellent information on how to find information on investing over the Internet. We noticed there was a good deal of general, non-Net related information included as well.

Investment club. If you want to invest by starting or getting involved in an investment club and need more information on what to do, or what the benefits are, read *The Investment Club Book,* by John Wasik, published by Warner Books. This is an easy-to-read, easy-to-follow book with good information on investment clubs and how to choose investments.

Direct stock investing. If you're specifically interested in investing in stocks directly and need more information, peruse *How to Make Money in Stocks,* by William J. O'Neil, founder of the *Investor's Business Daily,* published by McGraw Hill. This book doesn't give you specific "hot" stocks to buy, but it's an excellent resource for learning more about what things to know and consider when buying stocks directly.

Mutual funds. If you are going to focus specifically on investing in mutual funds, there are quite a few books with information on this topic. *Getting Started in Mutual Funds,* by Alan Lavine, published by John Wiley & Sons, offers information on the basics of mutual fund investing; it also compares different types of funds and presents their returns. *How Mutual Funds Work,* by Albert J. Fredman and Russ Wiles, published by the New York Institute of Finance, is more intensive and requires the reader to want to take the time to understand the material presented.

Associations

The American Association of Individual Investors (AAII). 625 N. Michigan Avenue, Chicago, IL 60611; toll-free number: 800-428-2244; Web site: www.aaii.com. The AAII is an independent nonprofit organization formed in 1978. To help individuals become effective managers of their own investments, the AAII provides publications, seminars nationwide, home study texts, educational videos, and local chapters that focus on investing and investment techniques.

Most of the 175,000 members of the AAII are experienced investors with substantial sums to invest, but they do have programs geared to the newer investor who is just beginning to build wealth.

The annual membership fee to the AAII costs $49 and entitles the member to receive the *AAII Journal,* published 10 times per year which provides information and how-to articles on investment fundamentals (it does not recommend specific investments). Members also receive *The Individual Investor's Guide to Low-Load Mutual Funds,* a 1,000 page reference book providing data on more than 850 low-load mutual funds, a yearly tax planning guide, *The Discount Broker Survey* and *Guide to Dividend Reinvestment Plans,* and reduced fees for seminars and educational publications.

Mutual Fund Education Alliance. Dept. 0148, P.O. Box 419263, Kansas City, MO 64193-0148; 816-454-9422; Web site: www.mfea.com. The Mutual Fund Education Alliance is an association providing information about mutual funds designed to help investors who want to make their own investment decisions and purchase funds directly, without brokers and costly fees.

For $19.50 you receive the *Complete Mutual Fund Investor's Kit* containing a 60-page educational book and a copy of the 236-page *Investor's Guide to Low-Cost Mutual Funds.* This guide also is available separately for a cost of $15. It includes information on nearly 1,000 funds and services from 41 no-load mutual fund companies.

National Association of Investors Corporation (NAIC). P.O. Box 220, Royal Oak, MI 48068-0220; 248-583-6242, Ext. 114 (to join); 248-583-4880 (fax); Web site: www.better-investing.org. The NAIC is a nonprofit educational organization founded in 1951. It offers membership on an individual, lifetime, or investment club basis. Costs range from $39 for an annual individual membership, to $575 for a lifetime membership. Annual club memberships are $35 plus $14 per year/per member.

The NAIC provides a number of services including a monthly magazine, *Better Investing,* a guide *Starting and Running a Profitable Investment Club,* investor information reports (or "green sheets") that give information on companies in which you might be considering investing, access to regional councils, and discounts on books and magazines related to investing.

The NAIC also offers a Low-Cost Investment Plan that allows a member to begin with a small monthly investment and invest in as little as one share of stock from a selection of more than 150 companies.

Glossary

This glossary is a bit different from some others you might have seen. Not only will it tell you what investment terms mean to ordinary people as well as to the pros, but it also will tell you why the terms are important to your decision-making process. We've included many of the terms used throughout this book, but because we know you're bound to use other resources out there, we've also included terms you're likely to run into elsewhere in your investment adventures.

Some of the terms even sound a little silly. *Bottom-up,* for example, sounds more like a toast than a way to evaluate stocks. *Efficient frontier* is another one of our favorite terms. Sounds like it has something to do with outlet-shopping in Arizona, doesn't it?

So, enjoy learning about these strange-sounding investment terms. Imagine that you are taking a trip abroad and are going to be faced with speaking in a totally different language. And think about how much fun it will be to surprise the natives with how much you know their language when you get there!

What the pros say . . .	*What this means to ordinary people . . .*	*How this matters to your decision-making process . . .*
asset allocation	The process of selecting different types of investments from different asset classes, based on their risk and return characteristics, and using them together to create a portfolio of investments.	This is an important concept. The goal of this strategy is to limit risk and improve the potential for return. Once your goals are set, you need to select a few different investments to give yourself a greater chance of meeting your financial targets.
A.M. Best's rating	A rating firm that evaluates the soundness of insurance companies. The top rating from Best's Rating Service is A+.	If you are going to buy insurance, invest in an annuity, or directly in insurance stocks, you should research the financial soundness of the insurance company.
after-tax real rate of return	This figure represents the *actual* amount of money that an investor is able to keep from income and capital gains earned on an investment, after taxes and inflation have been taken into consideration. Only the earnings after inflation are considered to be "real" investment gains.	It's very important to know how much money you actually keep from investments you've made. It's also important to be aware of inflation, because it can eat away the gains you've made.
aggressive	An individual investment (i.e., stock, bond, or mutual fund) or a portfolio (combination) of investments that gives the investor a greater possibility for higher investment reward and, at the same time, has a higher potential risk than investments considered to be conservative or moderate.	Most people should have some percentage of their money invested in a fund, or funds, considered to be aggressive. Few people should make decisions that involve *only* aggressive investments.
alpha coefficient	A number value that quantifies the difference between	This is very important if you want to impress your friends

What the pros say . . .	*What this means to ordinary people . . .*	*How this matters to your decision-making process . . .*
	the actual return and expected return. Expected returns are predicted by the return of the market overall and the beta of the security.	at your next cocktail party with your investment expertise. Unless you want to look at very technical measures of risk, this is not a number to pay a lot of attention to. It simply indicates the relative riskiness of individual securities.
annuities	Annuities are a type of investment product that provide regular payments for a future period of time. Annuities allow interest and earnings to grow tax free until they are withdrawn. Insurance companies develop and sell annuity products, but they can also be purchased through banks, mutual fund companies, or independent financial planners.	If you have maxed out your contributions to 401(k) and other retirement plans and made IRA contributions, and you are still looking for a tax-deferred investment, annuities may make some sense. Watch out for high fees, though. Annuities can be an expensive way to invest.
asset class	Different types of investments are grouped into asset classes. The three primary asset classes are stocks, bonds, and money market instruments.	In order to be able to choose different investments, you must know which asset class they fall into.
asset-liability matching	This is the idea of balancing debt and equity. All financial decisions take this into consideration at some level. An example would be choosing to take out a loan for your vacation (increase your debt = liability) or choosing to pay cash for the vacation (decrease your assets = cash). Always	It's extremely important to understand this concept—knowing how much debt you can handle is absolutely critical to your ability to make good financial choices for yourself. Be sure you don't take on any debt you can't handle.

What the pros say . . .	*What this means to ordinary people . . .*	*How this matters to your decision-making process . . .*
	consider your ability to repay debt, current interest rates, your current and future earning power, and how comfortable you are taking on more debt.	
bank trust department	A bank department that administers trusts and guardianships and settles estates. It manages investments for large accounts, generally $300,000 or more.	Investors with large sums of money can choose to go to a bank and set up a trust account to manage their money. If you do this, we advise you to remain involved in the investment decisions made for your account.
basis point	A basis point is equal to 1/100 of 1 percent. Investment fees and investment performance can be expressed as basis points.	This is one of those fun things to know about because investment people love to throw around jargon like this, but it's not particularly useful for your decision-making process.
before- and after-tax return	Profitable investments will always create tax bills for investors. Looking at the return before and after taxes will indicate the amount of money you'll actually keep after you pay taxes. The before-tax return shows how well the investment's portfolio manager did for you with that investment; the return after taxes is what you actually get to put in the bank.	You will always need to take taxes into consideration when you make investment choices. The good news for you—and for the government—is that the more your investments earn, the more taxes you'll pay.
beneficiary	A beneficiary is someone who will inherit the value of your investment account (or insurance policy) if you die. Also, when trust accounts are estab-	When you set up investment accounts, you'll need to designate a beneficiary.

What the pros say . . .	*What this means to ordinary people . . .*	*How this matters to your decision-making process . . .*
	lished, the beneficiary is the person for whom the money is managed.	
beta coefficient	A measurement of the change in price of a single stock relative to the change in the stock market overall. A stock with a beta of 1 moves with the market. Stocks with betas greater than 1 are considered more volatile than the market overall, and stocks with betas less than 1 are less volatile than the market overall. So a stock with a beta of 1.5 would show a gain of 15 percent if the market moved up 10 percent (10% × 1.5 = 15%).	This is another one of those terms used to impress friends and family at cocktail parties. Again, beta is a fairly technical measure of risk for stocks and not something to spend a lot of time worrying about.
Black Monday	October 19, 1987. The Dow Jones Industrial Average plunged a record 508 points in one day, after declining sharply a few times the previous week. Experts attribute the drops to investors' concerns about inflated stock prices, the federal budget and trade deficits, and activity in foreign markets.	It's important to understand what happened on Black Monday and to know that investors who sat tight have regained all their losses and then some. No expert knows for sure when a big drop is coming (or a big increase for that matter!).
bonds (corporate and government)	Bonds can be redeemed before their scheduled maturity date. The issuer has to pay the bondholder a premium price if they do "call" the bond back. This will usually happen when interest rates have fallen so much that it is less expensive for the issuer to issue new	Often considered the middle road between ultra safe cash and riskier equities, bonds offer predictable income with some volatility.

What the pros say . . .	*What this means to ordinary people . . .*	*How this matters to your decision-making process . . .*
	bonds, at a lower rate to borrow the money they need.	
bottom-up, top-down, approach	Portfolio managers typically use either a top-down or a bottom-up approach to investing. Some use both. Top-down investors look first at big-picture factors, such as the performance of industries and sectors, and then evaluate individual stocks. Bottom-up managers tend to look first at individual companies' securities and then evaluate the bigger picture.	When you look at the way different portfolio managers approach investing, it's important to know how they view the stock market.
bull investor	An individual who thinks stock prices are going up. A bull investor can be optimistic about the prospects for a particular stock, bond, commodity, industry, or the market in its entirety.	"Bullish" investors make more optimistic decisions than someone who sees less hope for increases.
buy/sell discipline	Investment managers need to decide when they will buy and sell individual securities in their portfolios.	Picking the right investments is just one part of the equation; you should be sure your portfolios won't hold on to investments that have soured, too.
capital gain	When you sell an asset for more than you paid for it, you realize a capital gain. Capital gains can be short or long term.	Capital gains are one of the ways investments increase in value and have tax implications.
churning	The practice of trading securities for the purpose of generating commissions. This is an illegal activity under the SEC rules.	If you use a broker, always be aware of what is happening in and with your account.

What the pros say . . .	*What this means to ordinary people . . .*	*How this matters to your decision-making process . . .*
common stock	A unit of ownership in a public corporation. A common stockholder is entitled to vote on the selection of directors and other company matters of significance, as well as to receive dividends (when paid) on stock holdings. If a company goes bankrupt, or is otherwise liquidated, the common stockholder stands in line behind secured and unsecured creditors, owners of bonds, and owners of preferred stock.	Common stocks are the kinds of stocks most investors buy. It's very important to know which type of stock you are buying as well as the company you are investing in.
compound interest	Interest that is earned not only on your initial principal amount, but also on any interest that has previously been earned on the investment. Interest can be compounded daily, quarterly, monthly, or annually.	Compounding is a very important concept with great benefits. The earlier you begin to save and invest, the more time your money will have to make money on itself!
conservative	An individual investment or portfolio of investments that offers less potential for high investment returns and at the same time a lower potential level of risk.	Conservative investments are a good place to put money if you want to limit risk, but still have an opportunity for growth. Most people should have some percentage of their assets invested conservatively. Few people should make decisions that involve only conservative investments.
Consumer Price Index (CPI)	A measure of change in the prices consumers pay for various basic items such as housing, food, transportation, and electricity. The United States	As you spend more time in the investment world, you'll hear terms like CPI quite a bit. It's one of the many indicators that we watch to get a sense

What the pros say . . .	*What this means to ordinary people . . .*	*How this matters to your decision-making process . . .*
	Bureau of Labor Statistics conducts a monthly survey to determine the CPI. Oftentimes, pension and employment agreements can be tied to CPI to protect the beneficiary against inflation. If the CPI goes up, benefits go up and their purchasing power, in theory, stays the same.	of where different markets for investments may be heading. The best approach is to establish a plan for saving and investing and stick to it, no matter what the different indicators are doing.
contrarian investor	An investor who does the opposite of what most investors are doing at any particular time.	You may find a mutual fund that takes a contrarian approach to investing. Some investment advisers focus on securities that are out of favor, indicated by a low price-earnings ratio relative to their peers in their market or industry. Like so many other approaches to investing, contrarians are right sometimes and wrong other times!
corporate bond	A form of debt issued by a private corporation to raise money. Corporate bonds are different from municipal or government bonds in a few ways; they're taxable, their par value is $1,000, a company's bonds come due at the same time (called a term maturity), and they're traded on major exchanges.	Corporate bonds have different features and benefits from government bonds. Government securities are backed by the government entity that issued them.
correlation coefficient	A measure of how two or more different investments perform under similar market conditions. If the correlation	This is a technical measure of how different investments will perform relative to one another. Using common sense,

What the pros say . . .	*What this means to ordinary people . . .*	*How this matters to your decision-making process . . .*
	coefficient between two investments is a low number, it means that they are not expected to react in a similar way, and it's likely that you can improve your total investment return by investing in both securities, without taking on more risk. Investments that are expected to do the same thing at the same time have correlation coefficients of 1, and together they would not give you a diversified selection of investments. Investments with negative correlation coefficients are expected to move in opposite directions.	you can easily choose investments that perform differently from one another to achieve asset allocation or diversification without knowing their correlation coefficients.
coupon	The interest rate on a debt security, like a bond, that the issuer of the security agrees to pay to the holder of the security until the maturity date. It's usually expressed as an annual percentage of face value. A bond that has a 10 percent coupon pays $10 per year every $100 of face amount.	If you invest in a bond or other debt security, it's imperative to know the interest rate you are earning.
custodial account	An account that a parent or other adult as trustee creates for a minor (a person under age 18) at a bank or investment firm. Minors can't authorize any securities transactions without the approval of the account trustee.	This is an investment account to consider for the important children in your life. Remember that you still will need to select the investments that go into the custodial account.

What the pros say . . .	What this means to ordinary people . . .	How this matters to your decision-making process . . .
debt instrument	A written promise to repay a debt. Bills, notes, bonds, and certificates of deposit are all examples of debt instruments.	Fixed-income investments are debt instruments. If you diversify your portfolio, you're bound to have some debt instruments.
debt/credit	Money that you owe to others is generally referred to as debt. Credit is the amount of money that is available to you to borrow.	This matters a lot—before you can begin an active investment program you should clear most of your debts. Few investments earn as much return as you pay in credit card interest, for example.
disclosure	Information companies release about themselves that might influence an investor's decision to buy or sell their stocks or bonds. Disclosure is required by the Securities and Exchange Commission and the stock exchanges.	You want to know all you can about a company before you decide to invest in it—and you want to make sure you understand the information you receive.
diversification	The process of choosing a number of different investments with different levels of risk and expected returns within your investment portfolio. Without diversification, investors would choose just one investment.	This is an important concept—simply the process of putting a number of different investment eggs into your investment basket.
dollar cost averaging	Investing a fixed amount of money into securities at set intervals of time. The investor accumulates assets by buying more shares of the investment when the price is low and fewer shares when the price is high. The overall cost of the shares is lower than it would be if a constant number of shares	This is a great way to invest money and accumulate assets. Effectively, you buy more securities when the price is low and fewer when the price is high. Not only are you investing on a regular basis—always a good idea—but your per-share costs are likely to save you money.

What the pros say . . .	*What this means to ordinary people . . .*	*How this matters to your decision-making process . . .*
	(rather than dollars) were bought at set intervals. Investment people sometimes refer to this as a constant dollar plan.	
earnings per share	Allocating a company's profit, after taxes and payments to preferred stockholders and bondholders, to each outstanding share of its common stock. A company with earnings of $5 million with 5 million shares outstanding would report earnings of $1 per share.	Earnings are a measure of a company's health and growth. This is a piece of information that you want to have before you invest in a company's stock.
efficient frontier	A graph or picture of the risk and reward relationship of a particular investment portfolio. An efficient frontier chart has risk on one axis and reward (return) on the other, and inside the graph it shows where a particular mix of investments fits. The "frontier" is the part of the chart that shows where the best possible mixes of risk and reward are located, where you can expect the greatest reward without assuming an undue amount of risk. An efficient investment portfolio will be very close to the efficient frontier on the chart.	You guessed it—another one of those cocktail party terms. This idea is important, though, because it is a way to express how well an asset allocation strategy is actually performing or is expected to perform. If you use a financial adviser, you may see something like this done for your portfolio.
emerging markets investments	The stocks or bonds of companies in developing countries outside the United States. Some current examples include, but are not limited to, Latin America, Asia, and India.	Companies in developing countries offer investors some of the greatest opportunities—and the highest levels of risk. Be sure you are comfortable with high levels of risk if you choose this type of investment.

What the pros say . . .	*What this means to ordinary people . . .*	*How this matters to your decision-making process . . .*
family of funds	A group of mutual funds managed by the same investment management company. Typically, each fund operates with a different investment objective. Often, investors have the convenience of being able to switch easily between funds in the same family with no charge.	From a cost perspective, this is an attractive option, provided there are enough good, diversified funds in the "family." Keep in mind that even though there may not be fees to switch funds, there can still be tax implications. Also, mutual fund supermarkets have created "virtual" mutual fund families, offering the services associated with a fund family, but with lots more mutual funds from different companies.
fiduciary	A person or a company holding assets in trust for someone else (the beneficiary). A fiduciary is charged with investing wisely on a beneficiary's behalf and must have sole regard for a beneficiary's interest when making investment decisions.	Be aware that most states have laws prohibiting a fiduciary from investing your money for their personal gain.
growth stocks	Stocks whose companies have experienced faster than industry average growth in earnings and are expected to continue to grow rapidly.	If you are looking for investments that will grow over time, growth stocks are something to consider.
index	A measure of change in a financial market. The Standard & Poor's 500 index measures the performance of 500 widely held stocks. There are many other indexes that measure different investment markets and industries. Most investments are measured by how well they perform in relationship to the performance	Indexes are a framework for understanding how well an investment has done over time, the best predictor of its future behavior. When you choose investments, it's helpful to see how they've performed compared to the index that they are measured against. But remember, as the fine print says, past perfor-

What the pros say . . .	*What this means to ordinary people . . .*	*How this matters to your decision-making process . . .*
	of the index that most closely resembles their investment style.	mance is no guarantee of future results.
inflation	The increase in the cost of the things we buy over time. Inflation has been about 3 percent annually for the last few decades.	This risk can be overlooked in investment decision making. Your money is only worth what it earns, above the rate of inflation. An investment that returns 5 percent when inflation is 3 percent gives you just a 2 percent gain (not counting taxes and fees, of course).
international	Stocks or bonds of non–U.S. markets. An international fund invests most or all of its money outside of the United States, while a global fund includes investments in the United States in addition to overseas investments.	International investments are an important part of a complete investment program. Given the importance of other countries to our economy, our global participation as investors is very important.
investment style	Style is the approach a professional investment manager uses in selecting individual securities for a portfolio. Growth managers tend to look for companies that are expected to show rapid, sustainable revenue and earnings growth. Value managers look for stocks they think the market has not fully valued based on the company's fundamentals or appear to be "cheap" when compared to competitors' stocks or other financial indicators. Many managers incorporate elements of both approaches.	When you choose a mutual fund, it is very important to know how the portfolio manager will choose the individual securities for the portfolio. You may want to diversify your portfolio by investment management style, in addition to asset class, because different styles do perform differently in similar market conditions. Keep in mind that two growth managers can have two different approaches to selecting stocks.

What the pros say . . .	What this means to ordinary people . . .	How this matters to your decision-making process . . .
liquidity	The ability to turn investments into cash quickly.	You should always hold a reasonable sum of money in liquid investments in case of emergency. The rule of thumb for a cash stash is generally six months of living expenses.
load	A sales charge paid by investors buying shares of a "load" mutual fund, or other investment that charges sales expenses to investors. Loads can be front-end or back-end.	It's very important to know any and all fees and sales charges associated with making an investment.
market capitalization ("cap")	The value of a company measured by the market price of its stock multiplied by the number of outstanding shares of stock. Caps are usually divided into three categories: small, mid, and large.	As a general rule, the larger the company's capitalization, the more stable the stock is expected to be.
maturity	The date that a bond or other type of loan becomes due.	The amount of time that a bond is expected to exist, its maturity, is one factor in setting the rate of interest it will pay. Generally, the longer the maturity, the higher the rate of return.
moderate	An individual investment or a portfolio of investments that offers a "middle-of-the-road" potential for investment reward and has a corresponding level of risk. Moderate investments are those that aren't classified as aggressive or conservative.	If you are "in between" goals, unsure of your time frames, or just plain uncomfortable investing aggressively, a moderate approach may make sense for you.
Modern Portfolio Theory	A theory about how to develop investment strategy in order to deliver the highest	Great cocktail party talk. Many of the important concepts we talk about stem from

What the pros say . . .	What this means to ordinary people . . .	How this matters to your decision-making process . . .
	possible return for a given level of risk, or the least amount of risk for a given level of return. The focus is on the statistical relationship among the various securities within an overall portfolio.	this theory, like diversification and asset allocation.
mortgage-backed securities	Securities that have mortgages as the underlying investments. Your return is based on how well the mortgages perform. If too many people or institutions don't pay their mortgages on time, or at all, the total return will be less than expected.	These are part of the universe of fixed-income investments. Until fairly recently, there was no market in these securities; now they are a big business on Wall Street.
municipal bond	A form of debt issued by a state or local government entity. The proceeds from the bond can be used for general governmental needs or special projects. Most municipal bonds are exempt from federal taxes and from state and local income taxes in the state issued.	These are particularly important to investors seeking to reduce tax bills.
mutual fund	Technically, mutual funds are investment companies established for the purpose of investing money from lots of different investors. They can invest in stocks, bonds, options, commodities, or money market securities in the United States and/or abroad. The fund earns fees for their professional management of investors' money.	Hands down, the most popular investment vehicle around. Mutual funds have made it very easy for people to start investment programs, and the number of choices available today is astounding.

What the pros say . . .	*What this means to ordinary people . . .*	*How this matters to your decision-making process . . .*
portfolio	A group of investments belonging to a person or entity. Think of a portfolio of investments as the pie dish that holds all of the different pieces of pie. Each investment is a slice of the pie.	It is very important to think of all of the different investments you own as a portfolio. This will help guide your decision-making process.
portfolio optimization	The mathematical process of determining the best possible combination of investments to provide the greatest possibility of reward for the least amount of risk.	Leave this to the investment experts. It is not necessary to optimize a portfolio to make good decisions. If you're curious, an investment adviser may have software that can do this for your portfolio.
prospectus	A written offer to sell an investment that tells the specific facts about that investment. For example, a mutual fund prospectus will tell you what the fund is investing in, risks associated with the investment, portfolio manager track record and fees, and other financial information.	It's very important to actually read the prospectus when you are choosing an investment, despite the oceans of fine print. Call the company issuing it and ask about anything you don't understand. You deserve to understand everything in it before you invest your money.
qualified plans	Qualified plans are retirement and other plans that qualify for special tax benefits. These plans generally offer investors the opportunity for tax-deferred savings and include employer-sponsored retirement plans such as a 401(k)s. The money in qualified plans is called qualified assets or plan assets.	Qualified plans are a great place to save and invest. They generally offer both tax benefits and a number of investment choices.
real estate	Investors can buy individual houses, apartments, or commercial property, or they can invest in funds that buy real estate.	You already may own real estate. As you consider ways to diversify your portfolio, real estate may make sense for you.

What the pros say . . .	*What this means to ordinary people . . .*	*How this matters to your decision-making process . . .*
risk and standard deviation	Investment risk is the possibility of change in the value of an investment. Standard deviation is a measure of the degree to which a security's price will be different from the mathematical average. The higher the standard deviation, the more drastic the up or down swings in price will be. Stocks have a higher standard deviation than bonds.	At last—a real-life application for your statistics class. This measures the amount of fluctuation an investment is expected to experience over time. You can make sound investment choices without having this bit of data.
security	An individual investment—a stock, bond, or money market instrument—is called a security.	Your investment decisions will always involve some kind of security.
Sharpe Ratio	A measure of an investment portfolio's excess, or additional, return in relationship to the portfolio's assumed level of risk. The higher a portfolio's Sharpe Ratio, the better, because an investment has delivered more return than it really "should" have given the level of risk it assumed.	The whole idea of measuring return relative to risk is very important. You should always have a sense about where the investments you choose fall on the risk/return continuum. Because the Sharpe Ratio is a technical measure, it is not required for making good investment decisions.
stable value investments (cash, cash equivalents, and money market investments)	Investments with a high level of stability and accompanying lower expected level of investment risk. Some stable value investments offer a stated or fixed rate of return.	This category includes the very safest investments. Because it is important to have some liquid assets, or cash, in case of emergency, everyone should have some stable value investments. Depending on your goals, your portfolio may include some of these as well.
stocks	Ownership of a corporation represented by shares of the corporation's stock. A stock share entitles investors to a	Stocks are the asset class that offer the greatest opportunity for growth and the highest level of risk.

What the pros say . . .	*What this means to ordinary people . . .*	*How this matters to your decision-making process . . .*
	piece of the company's assets and profits. Stocks are generally considered to offer the best potential for investment risk and reward of any asset class. The two primary forms of stock ownership are common stock and preferred stock.	
total return	This is the combination of both current income generated by an investment and the increase (or decrease) in its original value. If one invested $2,000 and its value grew to $2,500, the total return would reflect the $500 increase in value as well as any dividends and income paid to the investor while they held the investment.	Account statements typically show the return earned by investments. Returns are important because they quantify investment growth, and they allow you to compare investments to one another.
value stocks	Stocks of companies that generally have undervalued assets but are expected to appreciate to their full market value over time.	If you are looking for an approach to stock investing that might offer a bit more stability than growth stocks, take a close look at some investments that focus on value stocks.
volatility	The change in the value of an investment. More volatile investments are expected to change in value a lot, while less volatile investments can offer more stability.	When you're developing your portfolio of investments, you want to have investments with different levels of volatility to ensure adequate diversification.
yield	The current income generated by an investment, most often used in conjunction with bonds or other fixed-income investments.	Because this is a measure of investment performance, it is especially important if you choose to invest in fixed-income investments.

Index